NANAJI DESHMUKH

About the Editors

Dr. Bishnu Mohan Dash, Assistant Professor (Senior Scale), Department of Social Work, Bhim Rao Ambedkar College (University of Delhi), engaged in promoting Bharatiyakaran of Social Work Education in India.

Dr. Mithilesh Kumar, Assistant Professor, and Coordinator (Teaching) in Mahatma Gandhi Fuji Guruji Centre for Social Work, Mahatma Gandhi Antarrashtriya Hindi Vishwavidyalaya, Wardha, Maharashtra.

NANAJI DESHMUKH
An Epitome of Indian Social Work

Edited by
Bishnu Mohan Dash
Mithilesh Kumar

CONCEPT PUBLISHING COMPANY Pvt. Ltd.
NEW DELHI-110059

ISBN-13: 978-93-88937-89-4

First Published 2021

Published and Printed by

Concept Since 1974

Concept Publishing Company Pvt. Ltd.
A/15-16, Commercial Block, Mohan Garden
New Delhi-110059 (India)
T : 91 11 25351460, 91 11 25351794
E : publishing@conceptpub.com; W : www.conceptpub.com

Cataloging in Publication Data--Courtesy: D.K. Agencies (P) Ltd. <docinfo@dkagencies.com>

Nanaji Deshmukh : an epitome of Indian social work / edited by Bishnu Mohan Dash, Mithilesh Kumar.
pages cm
Contributed articles.
Includes bibliographical references and index.
ISBN 9789388937894

1. Deshmukh, Nana, 1917- 2. Social workers--India--Biography. 3. Politicians--India--Biography. 4. Social service--India. 5. Rural development--India. I. Dash, Bishnu Mohan, editor. II. Kumar, Mithilesh (Assistant professor of social work), editor.

LCC HV40.32.N36N36 2021 | DDC 361.3092 23

Foreword

Social Work has an ancient history in the Indian tradition. On examining the vital elements of Indian society as found in the old scriptures of India, we find that social work is embedded in the life in India from the outset. When I talk of the 'Bhartiyakaran' of Social Work, then it does not mean Indigenisation or Indianisation. Being indigenous is different from being classic and Indianisation is related with a geographical jurisdiction. *Bhartiyakaran* is not localization. If *Bhartiyakaran* is understood to mean that the spatiality is to be amplified, then this interpretation is not correct. Instead, it is the effort and the enterprise to develop, invent and revive the lost methodology of community social work by understanding the true nature of Indian society and the eternal interrelationship between society and individual.

From that perspective, what is social work? Is social work a charity or a profession? Or a profession in which the charity is embedded, or a charity in which a profession and charity are reciprocal? The way Europe determined the nature of society after the Renaissance or Industrial Revolution, it is clear that it assumed that society is an enterprise and if society is an enterprise, then the actions of society are based on the intent of profit. Europe assumed that society is the outcome of a contract where individuals created it to protect their interests. In both ways, it is believed as an artificial construction. Construction is always based on intelligence. Is Indian society really like this?

The concept of society in India was neither based on contract nor based on purpose. It is neither based on utility nor a God-made creation. Indian society is neither based on utility nor based on purpose. The principles of the origin of society which Europe had built up in its dogmatics, and out of which the USA adopted the principle of purposefulness as the basis for the profession of social work is not useful in the context of Indian society. Indeed, over time, what began as an applied form of sociology and finally as an academic discipline, utterly independent of sociology, came to play a central role in all professional studies and this is the period when the Bhartiyakaran came to the foreground.

From the Indian tradition, what is society? Society is not dependent on the state. Society is not controlled and regulated even by the individual. It is controlled and regulated by *Dharma*. Indian sociology is the study of *Dharmashastra*. It is not the study of theology. Therefore, it cannot be understood by theology, and it was the biggest mistake of Indian society to understand it as theological studies. Due to which the original form of social work could not emerge, till independence. It did not appear before Gandhi that social work can have a theoretical background from the Indian point of view. It is a different matter that Swami Vivekananda presented all the theoretical grounds on which the social work later evolved and appeared in the form of *Swadeshi* movement in Bengal.

In the Indian context, Social Work is neither charity nor profession but its nature of human being, i.e. *Dharma* or Moral Code of Conduct of human being. When we want to reconstruct some norms for social work, without understanding these contexts, and build a society based on those norms, then there is a difficulty. Like state governments, many of the efforts made for social welfare proved to be unsuccessful because the social values were not in conformity with the social values of the groups for which they had strived. Without understanding social values and without understanding the foundation of the society, all the hard work that goes on does not go in the right direction.

Today the cases of a heart attack in India have been reduced, stress is not arising because the most sustainable social segment is supporting our society. Gandhi meant this kind of society when he talked about *Swaraj* or *Dharma*-based state of *Ramarajya*. Gandhi's *Swaraj* was the rule of society. Indian society can be autonomous where there will be less dependency on state and government, and the society stands for the underprivileged class, and guarantee their protection and welfare.

The life and work of Nanaji Deshmukh are most appropriate for addressing these concerns. He constructed the necessary foundation for this work in the form of Deendayal Research Foundation apart from making the first attempt of professionalization of social work in India. He worked relentlessly for poverty eradication, minimum needs programme, cottage industry and agriculture. He successfully carried out the social restructuring programme in more than 500 villages of Uttar Pradesh and Madhya Pradesh. Today, we know Gonda, Balrampur and Beed because of the intensive work of Nanaji. The present and future social workers need to learn a lot from the works of Bharat Ratna Nanaji Deshmukh.

In this backdrop, I hope that this book will be indispensable in spreading the work of Nanaji to every member of the academic and professional fraternity of social work.

I congratulate Dr. Bishnu Mohan Dash and Dr. Mithilesh Kumar for bringing out the first ever volume compiling the various contributions of Nanaji Deshmukh for academic purposes. I also wish all the officials of the Bharatiya Samaj Karya Parishad for their endeavour and wish them success in their mission of *Bharatiyakaran* of Social Work education.

Prof. Rajaneesh Kumar Shukla
Vice-Chancellor
Mahatma Gandhi Antarrashtriya Hindi Viswavidyalaya,
Wardha

Preface

> "Nanaji Deshmukh's stellar contribution towards rural development showed the way for a new paradigm of empowering those living in our villages. He personifies humility, compassion and service to the downtrodden. He is a Bharat Ratna in the truest sense!"
>
> —Prime Minister Narendra Modi (2019)

The book "Nanaji Deshmukh: An Epitome of Indian Social Work" is a compilation of chapters which discusses the contribution of Nanaji Deshmukh towards rural reconstruction. The book categorically presents the multifaceted roles of Nanaji Deshmukh as Rashtra Rishi, Great Social architect, Great social activist, politician, a social entrepreneur and an educationist. The book has presented the Nanaji Deshmukh's Chitrakoot model of social work and rural development, and his various contributions for the betterment of the whole society. Keeping in mind his various contributions to Indian society and particularly his model of social work, rural development, education, health care, community development, Nanaji has truly institutionalized volunteerism and professionalism in social work in India and deserves to be regarded as father of Indian Social Work.

In the introductory chapter "Nanaji Deshmukh: An Epitome of Indian Social Work', Shri Mukul Kanitkar has clearly presented justifications for declaring the birth anniversary of Nanaji Deshmukh as 'Bharatiya Samaj Karya Diwas'. He mentioned that Nanaji Deshmukh has institutionalized professionalism in social work in India. Prof. Siddegowda and Dr. Krishna have highlighted the Volunteerism initiative to serve the underprivileged around him and in his motherland by writing the novel chapter of rural self-reliance through his independent initiative of Chitrakoot experimental model that ushered in new sun rise into several darkened rural livelihoods and heralded India on world map as that of the contributions of Johannesburg Hero. Dr. Dash in his chapter 'Social Work Practice: The Nanaji Way' highlighted that Nanaji's Chitrakoot model of development is an important viable scheme to be replicated all over the rural areas of India to ensure sustainable community development. In Nanaji model of development, he has placed greater emphasis on mobilizing people at the grassroots level and ensured their active participation in the development process. His model of development emphasized on community participation, integrated services for holistic development in the fields of education, health, agriculture, etc. In her Chapter, Prof. Sehgal discusses the contribution of Nanaji Deshmukh in rural development. His contribution to rural reconstruction is unprecedented and has no parallel, hence needs an in-depth study by social work research scholars as a basis for developing indigenous innovative social work approaches and intervention strategies. He was a true champion of the rights of the weak and poor, especially of the rural and backward Bharat and it is our proud privilege to have his body of work, to draw inspiration from. Mithilesh Kumar and Rajan Prakash in their chapter "Integral Humanism as the Guiding Principle of Social Work" highlight that in a time when social work is using compartmentalised worldview of the system, integral humanism offers the path of universal humanism and brings out harmony and functionalism in the society. If the Social Work has to strengthen its root in the academic world this must be included in the curriculum with a broad emphasis on the perspective explained by Deendayal. Nanaji Deshmukh experimented with this worldview in Gonda and Chitrakoot and showed that it is not only theoretical but can be applied in the field too. New professionals can connect with the local examples more than that of unknown and alien society having no relevance in Indian society. This will also help the profession to get back its mission with a humanitarian nature of service; with the creation of self-reliant, self-sustained, self-fulfilling society. Dr. Charu in her chapter has systematically reviewed the available evidence-based literature on the model and practices of sustainable village development model of Chitrakoot. Ms. Dimple in her chapter has described the Social action model used by Nanaji at Chitrakoot with a mission to create a prototype of self-sustaining model of development based on the concept of 'Gram Swaraj'. Dr. Geeta Sahare in her chapter has discussed various contributions of Nanaji. She also highlighted that Nanaji was a great social activist and was a system builder on a truly *Bhartiya* system based on our cultural and spiritual values, tuned to the needs and requirements of the present situation. That is what, he attempted in Gonda, and worked in the establishment of mini *Rama Rajya* and conflict free society that is his real contribution. She also highlighted the contribution of Nanaji in politics and other fields in her chapter. Divyanshu Kumar and Kumar Satyam in their chapter have highlighted the concept and meaning of Sewa and also described the contributions of Nanaji in the empowerment of the rural people. Nipun Savarna and Amod Gurjar in their chapter argue that integral humanism as an Indic concept can pave way for the process of indigenization and Integral Humanism's philosophy can be a pioneer in the accomplishment of the goal of social cohesiveness. Tripathi and Dwivedi in their chapter has discussed the various roles and functions of Deen Dayal Research Institute and also highlighted Nanaji's life and his voluntary efforts towards the society. Verma and Prasad in their chapter have put forward the contributions and thoughts of Nanaji Deshmukh, as compliments to the current knowledge that forms the basis of social work practice. They have also highlighted the self-reliance campaign of Nanaji and his ideas of conflict free society. Prasad and Actovin in their chapter have highlighted the significant role played by Nanaji in setting the climate for the growth of Indian social work as a profession. Their chapter has also focused on the contribution of Nanaji Deshmukh as well as its importance in social work profession. Dr. Sujatha in her chapter has highlighted that Nanaji Deshmukh's social work models are effective tools to achieve *Gram Swaraja* and self-sufficiency of villages based upon ancient Indian Knowledge System and freedom-oriented people's participation in development process. The Constitution of India provides the base to work upon different viable efficient models. An attempt is made in this chapter to understand the Sustainable Development Goals, in the backdrop of Chitrakoot Model of Nanaji Deshmukh for sustainable village development and need and necessity of application of Nanaji Deshmukh model throughout India. Dr. Diyali in her chapter highlighted the importance of Nanaji Deshmukh model for chasing Swachh Bharat Abhiyan successfully in India. Dr. Jha in his chapter highlighted that the great social activist Nanaji Deshmukh's holistic model of sustainable development in the field of village rural development, tribal development, health, education, agroforestry and animal husbandry. In his chapter he has described that the Chitrakoot experiment of *Gramodaya* (village development) included structural training programme for the activist grooming them into professional social worker. Chitrakoot model for social work and practices was his great inspiration that he learnt from his torch bearer in the field of social work. His social work model, field-work and practices towards a holistic restoration of the soil, flora and fauna diversity in chain of villages area presents specific feat of eco-system that imprints the huge format of ecological services to the higher canvas of integral humanism. The book will definitely serve as a reference book to the teachers and students of social work, rural development, sociology and other allied social science disciplines. It will be extremely useful to practitioners/ policy-makers and researchers engaged in community development and social work.

Dr. Bishnu Mohan Dash
Dr. Mithilesh Kumar

Contents

Foreword by Prof. Rajaneesh Kumar Shukla v
Preface ix
Contributors xv
Prologue xvii

1. Nanaji Deshmukh: An Epitome of Indian Social Work 1
Mukul Kanitkar

2. Modern Sculpturer of Rural India: Bharat Ratna Nanaji Deshmukh 13
Y.S. Siddegowda and *VST Krishna*

3. Social Work Practice: The Nanaji Way 33
Bishnu Mohan Dash

4. Nanaji Deshmukh's Vision of Rural Development 42
Ranjana Sehgal

5. Integral Humanism as the Guiding Principle of Social Work 52
Mithilesh Kumar and *Rajan Prakash*

6. Chitrakoot Model of Sustainable Village Development 62
Charu Sethi

7. Social Action: A Replica of Nanaji Deshmukh's Chitrakoot Project of Rural Development 74
Dimple Mishra

8. Nanaji Deshmukh: A Great Architect of Conflict-Free Society 89
Geeta Sahare

9. *Sewa*, Social Service and Social Development—Nanaji Way 97
Divyanshu Kumar and *Kumar Satyam*

10. Integral Humanism and Social Work 115
Nipun Savarna and *Amod Gurar*

11. Nanaji: As a Paragon of Service in the District of Chitrakoot 123
P.K. Tripathi and *M. Dwivedi*

12. Nanaji Deshmukh's Approach towards Community Development 132
Surender Verma and *Sunil Prasad*

13. Nanaji Deshmukh and his Contribution towards Nation Building: A Social Work Perspective 140
Sunil Prasad and *Arul Actovin C.*

14. Sustainable Development Through Law: A Real Tribute to Bharat Ratna, Nanaji Deshmukh 148
J.K.L. Sujatha

15. Chasing Swachh Bharat Abhiyan Through Nana Deshmukh Way: The Visionary Social Worker 157
Chandrakala Diyali

16. Nanaji Deshmukh: The Great Visionary and Social Architect 168
Dr. Yugal Jha

Index 176

Contributors

Dr. Amod Gurjar, Assistant Professor, Mahatma Gandhi Fuji Guruji Centre of Social Work, Mahatma Gandhi Antarrashtriya Hindi Vishwavidyalaya, Wardha.

Arul Actovin C., Research Scholar, Department of Social Work, Pondichery University, Pondicherry.

Dr. Bishnu Mohan Dash, Assistant Professor (Senior Scale), Department of Social Work, Dr. Bhim Rao Ambedkar College (University of Delhi), Delhi and General Secretary, Bharatiya Samaj Karya Parishad.

Dr. Chandrakala Diyali, Assistant Professor, Amity University, Noida.

Ms. Charu Sethi, Research Scholar, Department of Social Work, University of Delhi, Delhi.

Ms. Dimple Mishra, Research Scholar, Department of Social Work, Indira Gandhi National Open University, New Delhi.

Divyanshu Kumar, Currently pursuing social work course, Dr. Bhim Rao Ambedkar College (University of Delhi), Delhi.

Dr. Geeta Sahare, Associate Professor, Department of Political Science, Lakhmibai College, University of Delhi.

Dr. J.K.L. Sujatha, Assistant Professor, Department of Law, Jyotirao Phule School of Law, Dr. B.R. Ambedkar University, Etcherla, Srikakulam.

Kumar Satyam, Assistant Professor, Department of Social Work, Dr. Bhim Rao Ambedkar College (University of Delhi), Delhi.

Dr. Manish Dwivedi, Assistant Professor (Social Work), CSJM University, Kanpur, Uttar Pradesh.

Dr. Mithilesh Kumar, Assistant Professor, Mahatma Gandhi Fuji Guruji Centre of Social Work, Mahatma Gandhi Antarrashtriya Hindi Vishwavidyalaya.

Mukul Kanitkar, National Organising Secretary, Bharatiya Shikshan Mandal, Nagpur.

Nipun Savarna, Currently pursuing social work course, Dr. Bhim Rao Ambedkar College (University of Delhi).

Dr. Pawan Kumar Tripathi, Assistant Professor (Social Work), J.R. Divyang University, Chitrakoot, Uttar Pradesh.

Rajan Prakash, Research Scholar, Department of Social Work, Jamia Millia Islamia, Delhi.

Prof. Ranjana Sehgal, Professor, Indore School of Social Work and Vice President, Bharatiya Samaj Karya Parishad.

Sunil Prasad, Research Scholar, Department of Social Work, Visva Bharati, Sriniketan, West Bengal.

Dr. Surender Verma, Assistant Professor (Guest Lecturer), Department of Social Work, Delhi School of Social Work, University of Delhi, Delhi.

Dr. VST Krishna, Chairman, Post Graduate Department of Social Work, Vidya Vikas First Grade College, Mysore.

Prof. Y.S. Siddegowda, Vice Chancellor, Tumkur University and President, Bharatiya Samaj Karya Parishad.

Dr. Yugal Jha, Associate Professor and Head, Department of Political Science, K.K.M. College, Pakur, S.K.M. University, Jharkhand.

Prologue

It gives me immense pleasure to see that Dr. Bishnu Mohan Dash and Dr. Mithilesh Kumar are bringing out a volume '**Nanaji Deshmukh: An Epitome of Indian Social Work**'. This is perhaps the first ever book which deals with the various contributions of ***Bharat Ratna*** **Nanaji Deshmukh** in the field of social work and community development with academic perspective.

India had a different perspective towards the term 'social work' traditionally. The social value system incorporated all important factors as a part of routine life which are being dealt under the academic stream of social work in the modern times. Perhaps this was the reason that the study of social work as a separate academic stream was introduced in India substantially late. It also took considerable time to get it popularised. The social work education thus was introduced in India a 'foreign' academic stream.

Indian social work education today is highly colonised and Euro-centric. It has not been able to address the problems of the Indian society neither it expresses the Indian ethos. The curriculum and suggested readings provided to the students are largely borrowed from Western universities. The social work graduates after completing their education from Indian universities become misfit to handle the country-specific social problems as they have been trained in Western paradigms.

With various changes and advancements in the society in recent years, it was realised that the social work education is going to play a major role in shaping the society. It also generated interest and curiosity among the youth and students opting for their career in social work are growing day by day. Hence, strong need is being felt to look at this stream from the Indian perspective.

This book categorically presents the contribution of Nanaji Deshmukh in social work and rural development. The book covers Nanaji's model of development in the field of rural development, community participation, advocacy, environment conservation and much more. In his social work models and practice, Nanaji was inspired by the vision of integral humanism and successfully implemented it in the field of social work. The Chitrakoot, Gonda, Beed, and Delhi models of Deendayal Research Institute are testimonies of his contribution in the field of social work and community development.

I appreciate the efforts of Dr. Bishnu Mohan Dash and his team to promote the Indian perspective of social work education as well as development of indigenous literature in social work education. I am sure the book will be useful to the students of social work and other allied social science disciplines.

Dr. Sachchidanand Joshi
Member Secretary, Indira Gandhi National Centre for the Arts (IGNCA), New Delhi

1
Nanaji Deshmukh
An Epitome of Indian Social Work*

Mukul Kanitkar

The struggle for contextualisation has begun and it is heartening to see that it is not only limited to Bharat (India) but has extended to the whole world. This movement is now based at the global level. Lord Krishna says in Bhagavad Gita: "युद्धस्व विगतज्वर-*yuddhasva vigatajvara*", meaning – Fight! But never let fury or rancour overpower you! This is an important area in which we are working. Fifty years ago in 1969, Bharatiya Shikshan Mandal was established to embark upon the work of evolving Indigenous Education System. Working in every field of knowledge is necessary for revamping the entire education system.

Bharatiya Shikshan Mandal has formed the Board of Studies at the national level in forty-three subjects and is working towards its mission. It has reached completion in the field of Psychology and has formulated complete integrated *Bharatiya* (Indian) curriculum, same as Social Work which has already been implemented in many universities. The curriculum of psychology has also been introduced as the UGC model curriculum. Former Vice-Chancellor of Mahatma Gandhi Antarrashtriya Hindi Vishwavidyalaya, Wardha Dr. Girishwar Mishra made huge contributions and wrote the textbook also. Similar work is being done for management education suitable for Choice Based Credit System (CBCS) for both

* Keynote address delivered in the National Conference on Nanaji Deshmukh— An Epitome of Indian Social Work, organised in Indira Gandhi National Centre for Arts, New Delhi on 11 October, 2019.

graduate and post graduate courses BBA and MBA. Along with the Western subjects, Indigenous topics have also been included. Indigenous subjects comprise of study of *Raja Yoga*, *Karma Yoga* along with the Management models of *Bhagavad Gita*, *Ramayana*, *Mahabharata* etc. It is a matter of honour that a few papers have been accepted and adopted at IIM Indore, IIM Calcutta. Along with social work, the movement for *Bharatiyakaran* has started in every subject such as education, entrepreneurship, economics, political science, sociology and also physics, chemistry, etc. Social work is the pioneer and leader as we have also accomplished the task of preparing the reference material after designing curriculum. The first textbook of the subject is being published in this seminar. This has to expand to twenty-thirty books by prestigious international publishers in the coming two to four years. The *Bharatiya* vision of study of society has to be established as *Bharatiyakaran* of social work by conducting proper academic research and study. Thus, the mission has begun but a lot of intellectual labour has to be done to take it to the final stage.

This is not a political struggle. The word 'ideological struggle' imposed by some is also improper as we do not accept the word 'ideology'. Nanaji Deshmukh, Mahatma Gandhi did not accept the word 'ideology'. They did not have ideology. This is the vision, not an ideology. We do not hold anything, the construct, concept – Ideology. This entire structure is Marxist, communist structure. Therefore, it should not be accepted, not even in word. It is a struggle of vision. The struggle between the idea of those who say—"only this is right, do not accept the rest", and those who say—"think about all". True liberal vision is "आ नो भद्रा कृतवो यन्तु विश्वत: *ā no bhadrā kṛtavo yantu viśvataḥ*" meaning, let the knowledge come from all over the world. The knowledge that comes from anywhere is welcome. There is only one condition, only one qualifier that it must be constructive, it should not be subversive. This is the struggle between the vision which welcomes whatever is constructive with the vision of 'what I say is only correct'. This is the struggle between the all-inclusive expansive vision and the *dhārā*—flow limited by political banks. Those who want to establish their domination by holding a particular viewpoint will oppose it because they feel challenged.

They feel that we are trying to end their established domination. We are not doing anything like this. We are welcoming them too.

Today there is a discussion on the contextualization of courses all over the world. This is being done in medical education. If MBBS is to be pursued in Bharat, it must have a Bharat-centric curriculum. If one is teaching medicine in Africa, then (s)he will have to teach by taking into account the local circumstances. Euro-American-centred study of medicine will be useful for doctors in America or Europe. This is a simple matter but if some people assume this as the challenge, and stand in opposition, then you might have to show the courage. The mission is basically yours and you have to lead it, with the tools of the modern world, with full research, not putting anything in context without originality and citation. We should not be emotional in approach. We will have to test ourselves over and over again because we are under the 'lens'. One slip and they will catch it and say—look at it, they are talking nonsense, rubbish. Therefore, we will have to test ourselves more than the established.

I congratulate the Bharatiya Samaj Karya Parishad because it has done wonderful work. It is an important thing that those who teach, study and carry research in social work are doing it cooperatively in an integrative manner, keeping things in correct perspective with professional standpoint.

Today, this seminar on Nanaji Deshmukh: An Epitome of Indian Social Work can become a huge turning point. Seeds of thought have come out of this fourth seminar. For the first time, a seminar was held at Bhim Rao Ambedkar College of University of Delhi. Discussion on this subject was started. The curriculum was prepared at Mahatma Gandhi Antarrashtriya Hindi Vishwavidyalaya. It was our final stage and in Tumkur, we implemented the resolution that sought to adopt it. Today, after this seminar at IGNCA, our entire struggle will debut in the actual field of action. Hence, more preparation is required.

Nanaji Deshmukh got Bharat Ratna. We did not ask for it. We had demanded to declare the birth anniversary of Nanaji Deshmukh as National Social Work Day. The government did not do that but gave him Bharat Ratna. Now our demand will be more credit worthy. The country is proud of the work of Bharat Ratna Nanaji Deshmukh, his personality and his amazing talent. Initially, he did the work of Rashtriya Swayamsevak Sangh, then became a thinker, after which he was sent to politics. One is 'sent' to politics in Sangh but those who wish to go are not sent. Those who do not want to go are sent. Deendayal Ji was also sent in this way and Nanaji was also sent like this. After that, he did the work of setting the ideal in politics with the same spirit of calm. The party in which he was at that time went far ahead which no one expected. At that time, all political parties got his guidance under his leadership as he was without any adversaries – 'अजातशत्रु' – *ajātaśatru'*. He was much respected in politics because of his principles and character. The meaning of the word 'चरित्र – *caritra*' (character), in Sanskrit, comes from the root *'cara'* – meaning behaviour. Arjuna asked a very wonderful question in *Bhagwat Gita*—"स्थितिधि: किं प्रभाषेत किमासीत व्रजेत किं- *sthitidhiḥ kim prabhāṣeta kimāsita vrajeta kim– How does a balanced person speak, sits and behaves?* While asking he did not ask only the explanation that who is called 'स्थितप्रज्ञ – *sthitaprajñ'*. He asked—how does he move? How does he sit? How does he wake? Here one is not evaluated on how (s)he thinks, delivers a speech, but on what they do. Nanaji's personality inspires us for how he behaved and used words for people of opposite thoughts. He said that after 60 years, a politician should retire from politics and become वानप्रस्थि *vānprasthi.* At 60 years, he left everything even though everyone said they needed him.

After Emergency, Janata Party was formed and came to power under the leadership of Jayaprakash Narayan. At this time of glory, Nanaji kept his word and left the world of politics. He said that it is an opportunity to do the real service of people. For this, he settled first in Gonda, and then in Chitrakoot to carry out the experiment. He did what he said. He institutionalized social work. We should have no hesitation in accepting that there was no concept of social work here, in ancient times. It is true. We had a sense of service, 'निष्काम सेवा, नि:स्वार्थ सेवा – *'niṣkāma sevā, niḥsvārtha sevā'* – Selfless Service.

There is a narrative of Sage Aushastipada in *Chhandogya*

Upanishada. Sage Aushastipada practices *Vaishwaanar Sadhana* (practice) and propagates it to everyone, which Sage Gautama calls most difficult and best *sadhana*. For those who have difficulty in reading the original Upanishadas in Sanskrit, we have Baba Hazari Prasad Dwivedi's astounding grace in the form of a Hindi Novel *'Anamdas Ka Potha'*. There is a very wonderful description of the *Sevarthi Sadhana* in it. Upon reading the *Anamdas Ka Potha*, you will see the wonderful nature of Aushastipada's narratives. This idea, which started with the practice of *Seva*, goes up to the selfless service. Mahatma Gandhi advocated making it the field of study. Before that, Swami Vivekananda institutionalized it. There was still no social work in the picture in the whole period, from the beginning to the establishment of Ramakrishna Math and Mission by Swami Vivekananda.

The institution of *Matha* was established to provide training for the work of 'Mission'. It is very clear. Not many devotees of Ramakrishna Mission read what is written by Swami Vivekananda's own hands. There is much difference between the two. Swami Vivekananda gave the name Ramakrishna Mission and sought to institutionalize the tradition of *Seva* in society. Till now, we believed that *Sannyasis* should be served. Swamiji said, "you go and serve". Sannyasis do go from village to village to teach them how the eclipse occurs.

"दरिद्र देवो भव, मूर्ख देवो भव – *daridra devo bhava, mūrkha devo bhava*" – *Let poor be worshipped, let ignorant be worshipped* – are the words given by Swami Vivekananda, which Mahatma Gandhi re-established as *'Daridra Narayana'* – *Poor as God*. It was still a matter of social service and the social work had not come in the picture. Social Work as a field of study had begun 90 years ago in the universities, but social work in India with the Indian perspective was not there. *Sadhana* and from *Sadhana* to *Seva*, which was reflected in the words of Swami Vivekananda. He kept the motto of Ramakrishna Mission as आत्मनो मोक्षार्थम् जगद्धिताय च – *ātmano mokṣārtham jagaddhitāya ca*", which means good of the world along with one's own liberation. Gandhi takes this further from service to politics, social policy and above all to the national policy and we should not forget, even it should not fade into oblivion that Savarkar did the same. After coming back from Andaman, he did the same kind of work for untouchability, social reform and social service. At the same time, there is a very long list of social reformers starting from Keshav Karve, Bharat Ratna Dr. Babasaheb Ambedkar. On one hand, the institutionalization of social service was being done by Vivekananda and Gandhi and on the other, Vinoba Bhave was taking this forward. Many big institutions were established which were devoted to the principle of *Sarvodaya*–Good of all. On the other hand, there was another stream of an endeavour like Seva Bharati, Rashtriya Seva Bharati, etc., inspired by Rashtriya Swayamsevak Sangh.

There are three things. To work for the society as a *sadhana*, to work for society as a service and to work for social reforms. But here we are discussing professional social work which is different from these three. It might not be acceptable in Indian culture to take remuneration for doing the work of the society. Aushastipada, Vivekananda and Gandhi might not accept, so the sage of the nation who tried to establish this tradition had to gently oppose his mentors and the man who did that was Nanaji Deshmukh. The man saw fifty years ahead of his time and thought that along with social change, the work of the society should be distinguished as a profession.

It is clearly written in our Vedas that the *Vaidya* should not charge fees because his knowledge and his collection are invaluable. You cannot devalue it by taking a fee. Therefore, in Bharat, it is said that *Vaidya* should not take money. He should work as service. It is written, if you treat with the desire of a return, it will not be effective. That will not be pious. No matter how much knowledge you have while preparing the medicine, if you think on its price, the medicine will lose its properties. If the *Vaidya* works without wishing for the welfare of the patient, then the treatment will not have any effect—it is in *Ayurveda*. But today, Medical Science is a profession. Likewise, to study the society in an organized way and establish the tradition of social service with a professional orientation is its *Bharatiyakaran*.

Social workers working in society, village or town may charge fees for it, but their vision should be liberal and devoted considering the poor as God. If this is to be brought in the curriculum, then we will have to evolve its Professionalism (Ethical Professionalism). For this, a similar kind of structure will have to be built. Its experiment was first conducted by Nanaji Deshmukh, with the foundation of Deendayal Research Foundation. In the seminar, we are discussing social work education, but the product of this education will have to practice the profession. Great Nanaji Deshmukh established social work as Practicing Profession. He did two experiments. One, it was not acceptable to the society as well as his mentors that social work should be done for remuneration. Nanaji did this revolutionary work because he was looking 50 years ahead. Practice means Professionalism, i.e. Professional social work from a *Bharatiya* point of view. The other novel thing he did was accepting married couples as *Poornakaliks* (full-time workers). He initiated *Samaj-Shilpi*. Those who are looking through the glasses of ideology will not understand the contribution of Nanaji Deshmukh. So, they will challenge the choice. To substantiate, they will argue that the work of Nanaji was social service, not social work. The same logic will apply to Gandhi also. This is the problem with ideology. Therefore, we want a vision—not an ideology.

Nanaji's work is different from that of Gandhi, Vivekananda and Teresa. It was Nanaji who introduced the tradition of social service of Aushastipada and Vivekananda as professional social work within a *Bharatiya* perspective. So, only the birthday of Nanaji Deshmukh can be National Social Work Day. He started a tradition that Deendayal Research Institute today is taking forward. Later, it took 20-25 years for full-fledged professional social work to start. He introduced it in 1980 and it took some time to be accepted after which it was adopted everywhere. Today, we need to study that institutionalized structure. Thus, as a reply to the objection of choosing Nanaji's birthday as National Social Work Day, all the aspects of his life are to be put forth. Bharatiya Samaj Karya Parishad should bring out all the aspects of Nanaji related to social work in the form of a small book along with a detailed biography.

Bharatiya Shikshan Mandal is engaged in contextualizing each discipline as *Bharatiya* way of life establishing it as guide to the whole world. That needs to be done in social work. We have to give this vision of the global standard not Western. I am saying 'global' because that is the established vision in this era. The goal of social work is to eliminate the social, economic and political inconsistencies in that vision. One goal is of the development and another of reform. You will understand the vision of Bharat when you will study the work of Nanaji. What is the ultimate goal of social work in Bharat? What is the ultimate goal of medicine in Bharat? It is not our goal to build a society without disease. Being healthy is a positive concept.

The ultimate goal of any profession is to eliminate the need for that profession. When Dr. Rajendra Prasad inaugurated Mahatma Gandhi Hospital Jodhpur, a wonderful statement was uttered which is immortalised in stone even to this day. He said, "Though I am inaugurating this hospital, I want to say that the need for a hospital in independent Bharat should finish." सर्वे सन्तु निरामया: – *sarve santu nirāmayāḥ* means—the way of living is such that each individual lives a disease-free life. In the same way, the professional goal of social work is to eliminate the need for service in society and build a self-sufficient society. Nanaji did that. He established a university in Chitrakoot. Before starting courses, he created a practical example of self-sufficient village. Villages, which require no courts, no police, where there is no fight and do not require anything from outside are self-reliant. From 10-15, the number of villages transformed on the model of Nanaji has today risen to 796. The *Bharatiya* ideal of Social Work is a self-reliant society. This is what Mahatma Gandhi said. This is what Vivekananda said. This is the whole notion of *Swadeshi* of Mahatma Gandhi that society should be independent.

I would add that even Marx talked of this—a stateless society. Self-reliant, stateless society was his ideal. Stalin and Lenin could not understand this. Therefore, they established a state-centred society. Hence, USSR disintegrated. China is also currently working in completely state-centric manner. It is working in complete opposition to Marx. This is what happens with ideology. Those with vision also examine themselves. Why did Rama desert Seeta? We can do a seminar on this subject. Only Hindus have the courage to examine their own Gods.

We find the basis of Marx's stateless society in the 'eutopia' of Plato and Aristotle. Here in Bharat also, we have the idea of a stateless society as *Dharma Rajya* in *Shanti Parva* of *Mahabharata*. Bhishma was lying on the bed of arrows. Bhishma tells Yudhisthira, "न राज्यं न च राजा, न दंडो न च दंडिका:—*na rājyam na ca rājā, na damḍo na ca damḍikāh*" which means that neither King ruled, nor any punishment needed. This is the ideal of stateless society. Yudhishthira asks, "How did the society run then?" Bhishma says, "धर्मेंनैव प्रजा सर्व, रक्षन्ति स्मा परस्परम्—*dharmenaiva prajā sarva, rakṣanti smā parasparam*". Marx failed but Bharat succeeded. Bhishma was not saying to Yudhishthir that it will happen; he was saying that it was so. Many times in the past, we have established such an independent society. This was said by Bhishma 5100 years ago in Kurukshetra, lying on a bed of arrows, some 100 kilometres from here, at Delhi the national capital. This is a historical fact, not a future ideal. Marx was saying that 'revolution' will happen, Plato and Aristotle were saying that utopian society will establish. Bhishma said to Yudhishthir, "Have done it many times, you also do it". That is why *Dharma* has to be understood. *Dharma* is not a matter of Religion. People make sense of *Dharma* in every village of Bharat. *Dharma* means duty, it has nothing to do with worship—*Dharma* of a father towards Son, towards the neighbour, *dharma* of the King towards the subjects. It is not a matter of religion – Hindu, Muslim, Sikh or Christian. It is a matter of duty. *Dharma* means conduct. That is why people call ethos as *Dharma*. What is in the conduct is the *Dharma* -धर्मेंनैव प्रजा सर्वा वर्तन्ति – *dharmenaiva prajā sarvā vartanti*".

When the goal of social work will be to establish this ideal and it will work to strengthen and establish mutual cooperation in the society, the vision of social workers will change. They will not look at society as inferior. They will work with the sense of devotion that God gave them the opportunity to serve the needy with empathy and compassion and not as problem solving. Work has been done in Bharat with this sentiment. Even though *Vaidya* takes the registration fees, but while checking the pulse, if he concentrates on whether the patient has given Rs. 100 or 200, then he will fail to understand the pulse. You will understand the *Vata, Pitta, Kapha* only when you forget everything and concentrate only on the pulse.

For this, you also have to forget yourself. In the same way, a social worker will succeed only when (s)he will be able to forget himself/herself and work with duty, with the sense of *Dharma*. The ultimate goal of this society will have to be adopted in methodology. Only then the *Bharatiyakaran* of social work will gain paramount value, it will also become global, as it is the global goal of self-reliant society. Should not the society of America be self-reliant? Should not the society of Africa be self-reliant?

Our DNA, our mitochondria, our blood is loaded with the energy of Aushastipada. If we do not explain to the whole world, then who will? If we are not able to convince them, we will not perform our duty to what the sage said—एतद्देश प्रसूतस्य सकाषाद् अग्रजान्मनः। स्वं चरित्रम् शिक्षेरन् पृथिव्याम् सर्वमानवाः—*etaddeśa prasūtasya sakāṣād agrajānmanaḥ/svam caritram śikṣeran pṛthivyām sarvamānavāḥ*"—which means that we are by nature, born to teach all the beings of this earth. Nanaji did it by his character, by his own conduct not from the text. We will have to write the texts too. In today's era, everything has to be done. All instruments have to be used, but in the final phase, we will be evaluated on the basis of our character. You will be the worker of Bharatiya Samaj Karya Parishad only when this value will reflect in your work. Same light that shone in Nanaji's life will glow from our lives also. "My life is my message"—Mahatma Gandhi said. This is the ideal of Bharat. Even Swami Vivekananda said that his life is an open book which anyone can read. Those, who will read the book of Vivekananda will also become Vivekananda. Not the book that was written by Vivekananda but the book of his character. If we assimilate Nanaji's character within us, then it will be social work in the true sense. What will be the procedure to establish the ideal of self-reliant society as seen by Nanaji Deshmukh? How will social work be done to achieve it? What will be its methodology?

Here, we have three things. The vision, the principle of the vision and the *Dharma* of the principle. *Dharma* or Conduct is important in every philosophy. What is the vision? What are its principles? You have to do the theorization. Nanaji did that too. He presented the theory of all the subjects of social service. Likewise, we will have to work on the theory of social work and its methodology etc. Then only the *Bharatiyakaran* will be possible in true sense. We will have to research, experiment, prepare case studies and document. It is a big task of documenting the phenomena in 796 villages and similar tribal areas. A lot of scholars will have to work.

I have seen fully independent villages of forest-dwellers in Arunachal Pradesh. Forest-dwelling life is ideal in our social life. Many tribal still live that ideal social life in Arunachal Pradesh. If someone marries in that particular area, there is a tradition that the whole village goes to the jungle, bring bamboos and build a home for the married couple. It is the responsibility of the village to provide house to every couple. What would an ideal community life different from this be? They have been living in this country for thousands of years. They are not aware of any texts. They do not know Sanskrit, but it is in their conduct.

One of our workers went to a school in Arunachal Pradesh. He arrived at the home of a student to dine after walking for two days. Distance is not counted in kilometres there, it is counted in time. They say that their village is far away, two-three days away. As the workers went, the villagers made vegetarian food for the first time. They made *kofta,* pulses and rice. A stranger in a shirt and pant became attraction of the whole village. While they were dining, someone peeped. When asked, the host said, "He is my brother." A girl came and he said, "She is my sister." This continued throughout the dinner. The astonished worker counted 56. He asked, "How many siblings do you have?" "Maybe some fifty or hundred, have not counted", was the answer. Our worker did not understand. The worker wrote in his experience that it was Bhagwati's grace that he did not ask the question that came to his mind—Were they all his 'real' siblings? We are the ones who understand the developed word and distinguish between the real and the cousin. Had he asked, he would have been the first to introduce the concept of real and the other to the village. There was no such notion in the mind of those forest-dwellers. For them, everyone was their real sibling.

This is *Bharatiya* vision—a self-supporting society not broken under the domination of modernity. It does not mean that the tribal should not develop or adopt the urban amenities. But with all these technological advances, keeping the spirit alive is the job of the social worker. Swami Vivekananda did that work. To preserve this way of thinking should be the goal of social work. This should be the vision of social work. We should strengthen this affinity. For this, BSKP has to be evolved into a family. That will be the right vision of social work. We are not against even those who are opposing this vision. Our vision is to embrace them too. For this, we will have to improve our strength. When your strength will improve, many people come to meet you.

I see the future that studying every subject from the *Bharatiya* point of view will become the vision of the world. We are working for this cause because our traditional education system is going to be the mainstream education system of the world. Only then *Bharat Mata* will be the *Vishwaguru*. Swami Vivekananda and Gandhi Ji had started it, we have to take it to the final stage.

We have become the world leader in *Yoga* in the form of the International Day of Yoga. This will also happen in Physics, Chemistry, Nuclear Physics. Everywhere, Bharat will not only become a leader but will also become a mentor and we will see all this happening in our lifetime. We will see all happening in front of our eyes. This work has to be done with faith. We have to do it with the sense of welfare, not hate. We do not believe in—us versus them. It was taught by Nanaji. He had friends across the party line. The communists also respected him and those who opposed him also had to believe that he had something unique. We have to bring the ideal of Nanaji in our character. On this Bharatiya Samaj Karya Diwas Day, we are celebrating the birth anniversary of the great Nanaji Deshmukh. The government may declare National Social Work Day. We have already done it. Why should we depend on the government? We have announced today in this seminar on behalf of the Bharatiya Samaj Karya Parishad. Rest, the government will follow.

2

Modern Sculpturer of Rural India

Bharat Ratna Nanaji Deshmukh

Y.S. Siddegowda and *VST Krishna*

Introduction

Nanaji Deshmukh (1916-2010) is a rare individual in the modern India who inherited the spirit of the Hindu culture which believed in the joys of sharing and charity. Serving the humanity has been the trait of his character and the spirit of his life. His voluntary services towards the welfare of the underprivileged have rendered material recognitions insignificant and humbled the men of great stature. His voluntary services have heralded a new Chapter of the Self-Reliance in the rural India with his independent initiatives at Chitrakoot on experimental basis. These initiatives not only ushered in a new beginning in the lives of the rural masses but also declared the appearance of the Johannesburg Hero on the map of the world.

The origin of his ideologies lies in the traditions of the indigenous spirituality of the Ancient Indian heritage which is called the *Sanathan Arsha Dharma*. Living in the villages, he spent all his vigor and youthful years in the service of the villagers and attained the status of a national sage, in other words he lived like a 'Rashtriya Rishi' promoting the welfare of the villagers as envisioned by Lal Bahadur Shashtri ji in his dictum ' Jai Kisan'. He considered that his services to the humanity are the offerings to the God as prophesied in Tagore's *Gitanjali*.

He had no time to struggle for upward mobility among the cadets and achieve higher ranks though he was known to be a leader with inherent natural charisma which he realized while working among the agrarian communities in India. Thus, his initiatives towards achieving the Green Consciousness and Animal supportive measures still shine across the borders of India. He didn't achieve the stardom overnight, nor did he aspire to be a celebrity. In fact, several opportunities knocked on his door to provide chances to climb the ladder of the success but he ignored the opportunities to dedicate himself to serve the lives of the poor who live in the dark sheds and huts who struggle to earn a day's meal observing the words of the great monk of India Swami Vivekanandaji who stated, "I will not allow even a dog to starve in this country…." He resembled the aura of Jyothiba Phule and Maatha Savithribhai Phule and he reinvented himself as a servant like the saint Pandit Rama Bai and a giant like the Madam Durga Bai Deshmukh.

He never aspired nor thought that he would be honoured with Bharat Ratna as he found solace in the grasslands and muddy villages in the agrarian environs to harness the animals. He could visualize the significance of the Chitrakoot initiatives, apart from his rural initiatives. Shriman Nanaji Deshmukhji went through the hurdles during his childhood similar to the difficulties faced by the former Prime Minister late Shastri Ji. However, he never failed to come out with the flying colours in his academic endeavours which were largely sponsored by the members of his family as he was ripped off the joys of being brought-up by biological parents. Hence, he acquired a personality to be the living emblem of the "Father of the rural lives".

A study of his personality reflects his life as described in the various verses of the *Bhagavad Geeta*. As the authors of this article would politely and humbly describe the life of Shriman Nanaji Desh Mukh with the first three *Slokas* of the *Bhagavad-Gita's* Sixteenth Chapter: *Daivasura Samvad Vibhag Yog* as mentioned below that he lived a life of tenacity, hard work and spiritual discipline. The following stanzas describe Shriman Nanaji Deshmukhji much better than the authors of this article:

भगवद् गीता, दैवासुरा संपद्विभागयोगम अध्याय श्लोक

16.1 श्री भगवानुवाच अभयं सत्वसंसुद्धि ज्ञानयोगव्यवस्थितिः दान
दमश्च स्वाध्यस्तप आर्जवम्
16.2 अहिंसा स्तयामक्रोध्यत्यागशान्तिरपैसुचम दयाभूत्वेष्वलोलत्वम
मारधावम ह्रिरचापलम
16.3 तेजहः ख्मादृति सैचमद्रोहो नातिमानिता
भवन्ति संमपदम दैवीमभिजातस्य भारता।

In reality, Sri Nanaji Deshmukh was ripped off those qualities that were unable to win him over ever in his social transactions, such as in the words of *Bhagavad Gita*:

16.4 दम्भोदर्पोभिमान्श्च क्रोदः पारुष्यमैवच
अज्ञानम चाभिजातस्य पारधा संमपदमासुरिम।

Thus, he remains as the "Ratna for our BHARATA Maatha" and the "BHARATA Ratna" no wonder garlanded to him, this impeccable stature of persona. This article intends to briefly trace the following:

1. उपास्यम : The Core adoration
2. उपादेयता : What was attained
3. उपादान : What was detached
4. उपाधि और : What was in dwelling, and
5. उपागतम : What is deliverable of the Nationalist persona Shriman Nanaji Deshmukh?

He galvanizes the strength towards the social engagement in the upliftment and services to the rural societies thereby he offers the fruits of Social Service that inevitably yield the Seeds for Social Work professionals initially and the Profession of Social Work in India in particular and the globe at large.

Let's understand the words of Shri Sathya Sai Baba of Puttaparthi, how he describes the treatment for the maladies of the modern living: (as "Neurosis be the fruit of Civilization" as Sigmund Freud has aptly spelt long back):

> परोपकारायफलंति वृक्षम
> परोपकाराय वहंति नद्य:
> परोपकाराय दुहंति गय:
> परोपकाराय इदं शरीरम्

Now let's travel through a few of the milestones in the life of Nanaji Deshmukh:

Let's accept:

> *The fruit never aspires to be forest*
> *but inevitably becomes,*
> *The River never knew it is going to be*
> *The great OCEAN*
> *but it leads to be ONE!!*
> *Early Morning the first Ray of the Sun,*
> *does never yearn to lighten the entire*
> *National boundaries!!*
> *But the day proves it!!*

Nanaji is not a name but an institution of yeomen's human services and the foundation for all Professional Social Work. In fact, the Departments of Social Work are the derivatives of the Vedic ideals. "Aathma Parabrahma" which intends to recognise the inherent potentials of the humans and the engineering of excavation of these innate potentialities laden with dignity and self-worth are the crux of the Professional Social Work and the human Engineering programme. Thus, Nanaji had laid the firm foundations for Professional Social Work through his deeds in his Chitrakoot experiment.

मैं अपने लिए नहीं, अपनों के लिए हूँ अपने वे हैं जो पीड़ित और उपेक्षित हैं।

These etchings on his abode of rural renaissance indicate the persona of Nanaji Deshmukh in brief. Whatever is said and done about Professionalization of Chitrakoot as an independent experiment by professionals, Shriman Nanaji Deshmukh remains an Ocean of Service to the humanity where the professions of different ideologies merge finally into the oneness of the ocean for the upliftment of the downtrodden and the needy. That is in the embodiment of the name called *Nanaji Deshmukh, the ocean of human development beyond the borders of the nations, spaces, cultures and contexts. Approaches do vary as the rivers do vary but finally do merge into the unison of Ocean: "Upliftment" for which the name of Sage of India Nanaji Deshmukh stands for eternally like* a pole star, a Dhruva Taara too.

> अविभाजितं देवं चरंते बहु वेषाणि
> बहुरूपिया भावितं ,चिन्तितेना चित्त
> चित्रणम सर्वम भावनोद्भवम यधापि
> नानारूपिणम नदिनाम सागरो गती।

Quoting the most prominent motivational literature of our times we can use the parlance of Nanaji to that of Richard Bach Jonathan Livingston "*the Seagull*" which was distinguished by its aspiration for excellence and the heights it reaches not just for existence but to create the distinction between existence and living for the society as Richard Bach puts it "*most Seagulls life consists simply of eating and surviving. Flying is just a means of finding food. However, Jonathan Livingston Seagull is no ordinary bird. For him, flying is the life itself. Against the conventions of seagull society, he seeks to find a higher purpose and become the best at doing what he loves*".... Richard Bach.

"All know that the drop merges into the ocean, but few know that the ocean merges into the drop..." Kabir Das—as said Nanaji is a drop where the Ocean of Human Service had merged proudly into his persona making India proud of his services.

Nanaji happens to be a fruit that he never knows it's being to be a forest in later updation and the river knows it be an Ocean but the fruit and river perform their natural responsibilities without expecting the foresthood nor the Oceanhood. "He was a paragon of simplicity, dedication and services and he was blessed with exceptional organizational skills" as our beloved Prime Minister Shriman Narendra Modiji puts it in one liner. 'Atma Nirbhar Bharat' was his motto of living.

He is a Bhagiratha having Jayaprakash Narayan and Mrs. Prabhavati as his Ram and Seetha maatha, and he enlivened the spirit of services of Hanuman. Deendayal Upadhyay was his spiritual mentor who carved him as a Nation builder. Dr. Hedgewar (Nanaji Sangh) and Apte ji have stamped on his services during the early years towards the upiftment of vulnerable communities.

His *Karma Bhoomi* is Jayaprabha village and he made it to be the reality of "*Vasudhaiva Kutumbakam*" through his bondage and attachment to the downtrodden lot of rural India. 10,000+Tharu Tribal children were his mirrors message to the world. Youth and Women Self-help Groups made him Indian Mohammud Yunus. Indigenous approach for *Swavalamban*, landing *Gram Swaraj* with his volunteers spanned among 500 villages spreading over Maharashtra, Madhya Pradesh, Beed, Nagpur, Delhi and Chitrakoot. The position of the General Secretary at Samagra Kranti engaged him in the revolutionary movement under the tutelage of Lokpriya Jaya Prakash Narayan and Mrs. Prabhavati on whose names he carved Jayaprabha village.

Nanaji etched a model of sustainable development in the village-economy of India. He is an embodiment of Welfare Economics as pioneered by Amartya Sen who promulgated that quality education has to be accessible, affordable and available to the commoners is the utmost priority for uplifting the downtrodden lots of India. He re-experienced the Bangladesh Model of Micro financing in India. His arsenals of services are targeted right into the core of education, health, self-reliance. He was the North Star born into Kandoli in Hingoli district on October 11, 1916 to bring peace and harmony to the poverty-stricken and war hit world. He was the fifth of his two brothers and three sisters. His noble parents are *Rahabai and Amrit Rao Deshmukh* who fondly named him *Chandika Das Amrit Rao Deshmukh but got renowned as Nanaji* in later years by his deeds and actions. His abode was a simple hut made of Bamboo facing Manasa lake of Jayaprabha gram. He passed away on 27th February,

2010, at the age of 94 with geriatric issues. His body was donated to AIIMS facilitated through Dadhichi agency.

On his BIRTH CENTENARY on 11 October, 2017, our beloved nation building Prime Minister Modiji repeatedly praised the deeds of Nanaji as an exceptional organizer and political consensus maker and who could motivate industrialists to the cause of rural development through his charismatic personality and live programme of GRAMODAY PARIKALP JAYAPRABHA village which later spread to Maharashtra, Beed, Nagpur and Delhi by covering a mammoth of 60,000 youth, 300 women into the Self Help Group initiatives focusing on the comprehensive development to provide access to education, health and economical self-reliance with focusing on *Swachha Bharat.*

10,000 of *Tharu tribal children* are all in smiles today as the gateways for being honoured with the Highest Civilian award of Bharat Ratna where his saga started in *Devipatan Mandal where he proved as a successful persona* in forging the political consensus. His passion for rural services motivated the Youth and Industrialists Social Causes and Rajmaata of Balarampur had gone to the extent of donating 50 acres of land to his noble pioneering works. He ultimately landed the Gandhian Gram Swaraj into the flesh and blood of rural India. The Tharu tribes were his reason to feel the inner joy and made him a towering public figure and invaluable personality, an Indian icon for organizational skills and leadership against poverty, hunger and the marginalized. He found that the strongest chain depends on the weakest link of Rural India. On Oct. 2014 celebration, Modi ji promulgated that Nanaji was an extremely inspiring soul of India.

He demonstrated the fighting spirit of winning the confidence of the public through democratic means by defeating Rajmata of Balarampur in 1977 elections and however he took *Sanyasam* from worldly achievement drive in 1978 with his legacy of 25 years of glittering leadership in the midst of offers at his feet to be the Minister in Central Government. He had to forego everything for his dreams on Janaki Nagar Gram Panchayat and for heralding the flag of Comprehensive Integrated approach based on rural self-reliance through his Chitrakoot experiment where he dedicated to Gau the Holy Cows and proved his love towards biodiversity and the spirit of rural transformation and the adoration and decorated with Padma Bhushan and Bharat Ratna by the Government of India are natural rewards for his dedication and the spirit of service and the rich legacy of infusing the self-worth and dignity to the rural India.

Bharat Ratna being received Posthumously by Shri Nanaji Deshmukh Family member...

Glimpses of Nanaji's Saga and Earthly Voyage: Early Life

Nanaji was born on 11 October, 1916 into a Marathi-speaking Deshastha Brahmin family at Kadoli, which is a small town in the Hingoli district. He worked as a vegetable seller to raise money for his education. He went to high school in Sikar, where the Raoraja of Sikar gave him a scholarship. He studied in Birla College (now BITS, Pilani)). In the same year, he also joined the Rashtriya Swayamsevak Sangh (RSS). Though born in Maharashtra, the fields of his activities were Rajasthan and Uttar Pradesh. The then RSS chief M.S. Golwalkar sent him to Gorakhpur (U.P.) as "pracharak" (full-time functionary). He rose to be the *Saha Prant Pracharak* of the whole of Uttar Pradesh (which has now become the eighth *prant* of RSS).

RSS Volunteer

Deshmukh became inspired by Bal Gangadhar Tilak and his

nationalist ideology, as well as showing an acquired interest in social services and activities. His family was in close contact with Keshav Baliram Hedgewar who was a regular visitor to Deshmukh's family. He could discern potential in Nanaji and encouraged him to attend RSS *shakhas*. In 1940, after Hedgewar's death, many youngsters inspired by him joined the RSS in Maharashtra. Deshmukh was among those who joined the RSS devoting their whole life in service to the nation. He was sent to Uttar Pradesh as a *Pracharak*. At Agra, he met Deen Dayal Upadhyaya for the first time. Later, Deshmukh went to Gorakhpur as a *pracharak* where he took great pains to introduce Sangh ideology in the eastern UP. It was not an easy task at that time as the Sangh had no funds to meet even day-to-day expenses. He had to stay in a *Dharmashala* but had to keep on changing *Dharmashalas* as no one was allowed to stay there for more than three days consecutively. Ultimately, he was given shelter by Baba Raghavdas on the condition that he would also cook meals for him. Within three years, his hard work bore fruits and almost 250 *Sangh Shakhas* commenced in and around Gorakhpur. Nanaji always laid great emphasis on education. He established India's first *Saraswati Shishu Mandir* at Gorakhpur in 1950.

When in 1947, the RSS decided to launch two journals *Rashtradharma*, *Panchjanya* and a newspaper called *Swadesh*, Shri Atal Bihari Vajpayee was assigned the responsibility of the editor and Deen Dayal Upadhyaya was made the *Margdarshak* with Nanaji as the managing director. It was a challenging task as the organization was hard up for money to bring out the publications, yet it did never dampen their spirits and these publications gained popularity and recognition because of their strong nationalistic content.

Mahatma Gandhi's assassination led to the imposition of ban on the RSS and publication work came to a grinding halt. A different strategy was adopted keeping the ban in mind and Deshmukh was the brain behind underground publication work by the RSS those days.

Political Life

When the ban was lifted and it was decided to have a political organization, Bharatiya Jana Sangh came into being. Deshmukh was asked by Golwalkar to take charge of Bharatiya Jana Sangh in Uttar Pradesh as its general secretary. In Uttar Pradesh, BJS gained strength from Upadhyaya's vision, Atal Bihari Vajpayee's oratory skills and Deshmukh's organizational work and it emerged as an important player in the state politics. Deshmukh always shared good relations not only with his party colleagues but also with his opponents. Gupta, who suffered many defeats at the hands of Deshmukh, yet continued to have great respect for him and called him 'Nana Phadnavis'. His relations with Dr. Ram Manohar Lohia changed the course of Indian politics. Once he invited Lohia in BJS *karaykarta sammelan* where he met Upadhyaya for the first time and this association brought the BJS closer to other socialist parties in exposing the Congress and its misrule. Deshmukh actively participated in 'Bhoodan Movement' started by Vinoba Bhave. Later, Narayan himself and Morarji Desai, who became the Prime Minister heading the Janata Party Government offered him the Cabinet portfolio of Industry, but Deshmukh spurned the overture. Deshmukh had won in the 1977 election held after revocation of the Emergency with a comfortable margin from Balrampur Lok Sabha constituency of Uttar Pradesh. When Narayan gave the call for "Total Revolution" Deshmukh responded by giving total support to this movement. He was nominated to Rajya Sabha by the NDA Government in the year 1999 in recognition of his services to the nation.

Social Work

After retirement from active politics Deshmukh then served Deendayal Research Institute that he himself had established way back in 1969. He did work towards the anti-poverty and minimum needs programme. Other areas of his work were agriculture and cottage industry, rural health and rural education. Deshmukh assumed chairmanship of the institute after leaving politics and devoted all his time to building up the institute. He was also instrumental in carrying out social restructuring programme in over 500 villages of both Uttar Pradesh and Madhya Pradesh states of India. He also published the journal "Manthan" (introspection) which was edited by K.R. Malkani for many years. Deshmukh did social work in Gonda (U.P.), Balrampur and Beed (Maharashtra). The motto of his project was: *"Har hath ko denge kaam, har khet ko denge paanee".*

He also established Chitrakoot Gramoday Vishwavidyalaya in Chitrakoot, India's first rural University, and served as its Chancellor. Nanaji implemented the philosophy of integral humanism to improve the living standards of more than 150 villages of Bundelkhand.

Landmarking Appreciation and Recognitions

He was awarded Bharat Ratna in 2019 (Posthumously) and Padma Vibhushan in 1999.

End of his Earthly Mortal Life

Deshmukh left his physical body on 27 February, 2010 in the premises of Chitrakoot Gramoday Vishwavidyalaya that he established. He was unwell for some time due to geriatric problems and had refused to be taken to Delhi for treatment. He bequeathed his body to *Dadhichi Dehdaan Sanstha* of New Delhi which was accepted, and his body was sent to All India Institute of Medical Sciences for medical research. His body was sent by road up to Satna, Madhya Pradesh, and hundreds of people and local residents accompanied this last procession to Satna. From Satna, his body was carried by a chartered plane to New Delhi. In New Delhi, his body was kept for few hours at Keshav Sadan (Delhi headquarters of the Rashtriya Swayam Sewak Sangh), and after that the body was donated to AIIMS with the help of *Dadhichi Dehdan Sanstha.*

Shri Nanaji Deshmukh—Founder, Deendayal Research Institute

Nanaji's life is a mission and his mission is his life. He made up his mind while he is still in his teens to dedicate himself to the service of our motherland. Since then he never looked back nor has any time for a sojourn in his life's pilgrimage. At the age of ninety two years he stands as a beacon of light to the multitude of Indians and as an inspiring source for lakhs if not millions of people that came into his contact through the programmes conceived and organized by this stalwart of our nation. The ordeals he went through be it in the pursuit of social work, political activities or during and after the total revolution movement of Loknayak Jaya Prakash Narayan, never deterred him to deviate from his life's mission. We are much aware that it is not possible to comprehensively picturize the activities and achievements of Sri Nanaji. What we presented here in black and white can only be a part but sure enough to understand the picture of his activities on our nation's canvas. Very few know that even at the age of 92 years he worked 14-16 hour a day for the success of the programmes on hand designed by him for the upliftment of rural masses of India.

Milestones of a Versatile Personality

1. Name: Nana Deshmukh
2. Date of Birth: 11th October, 1916 Age: 94yrs.
3. Positions held
   (i) Member Rajya Sabha from 1999 to 2005. (Nominated by President of India)
   (ii) Founder, Chancellor, Mahatma Gandhi Chitrakoot Gramodaya Viswa Vidyalaya, Chitrakoot 1991-1994 (First Rural University in India)
   (iii) Elected Member of Parliament in the year 1977.
   (iv) Founder and continues to be chief architect of Deendayal Research Institute since the year 1968.
   (v) Managing Director, Rashtra Dharma Prakashan 1948-51. (This trust publishes the magazines *viz.*, *Panchjanya* a weekly and *Swadeshi*, a daily)

(vi) Founder of the chain of Saraswati Sishu Mandirs in U.P. in the year 1950. At present this is the largest chain of schools numbering 14,000 spreading all over India.

4. Distinctions

Milestone Year's in the Life and Living of Nanaji Deshmukh:

2008 — Chandrashekharendra Saraswati National Eminence Award for Community Development awarded by Kanchikamkotimath.

2008 — D. Litt. awarded by Mahatma Gandhi Chitrakoot Gramodaya University.

2006 — Samta Award, awarded by Shri Akhil Bharatvarsiya Sadhumargi Jain Sangh, Beekaner (Rajasthan). 2006 — Gyaneshwar Award, awarded by Gyaneshwar Vidyapeeth Pune, and presented by The Hon'ble Vice President, Shri Bhairon Singh Shekhawat.

2005 — Jhunjhar award, awarded by Jhunjhar Samiti, Pune.

2005 — National Mahatma Gandhi Award, presented by the Madhya Pradesh Government.

2003 — Jeevan Gaurav Puruskar, awarded by Chaturang Pratisthan, Mumbai.

2002 — Samta Award, awarded by Shri Akhil Bharatvarsiya Sadhumargi Jain Sangh, Beekaner (Rajasthan). 2001 — D. Litt. awarded by Bundelkhand University, Jhansi.

2001 — National Citizens Award, awarded by Justice P.N. Bhagwati, Hon'ble Chairman, U.N. Human Rights' Commission.

2000 — Doctor of Letters awarded by the Chatrapati Sahuji Maharaj University, Kanpur. 1999 — "Padma Vibhushan" awarded by the President of India.

1998 — Doctor of Letters awarded by Maharshi Dayanand Saraswati Viswavidyalaya.

1997 — Doctor of Letters awarded by the University of Pune, Pune. 1997 — Rashtriya Ekata Puraskar awarded by R.G. Joshi Foundation.

1996-97— Person of the Year awarded by the Rotary International.

1997 — Manas Sangh Sanman on the occasion of Sant Tulasi Das, 500th Birthday.

1995 — Scroll of Honour by the International Federation for Women in Agriculture—Presented by MS Swaminathan, President, IFWA.

1995 — Rama Sastry Prabhune Pratishtan Award.

He was awarded Bharat Ratna in 2019 (Posthumously) and Padma Vibhushan in 1999.

Work and Achievements

Shri Nanaji Deshmukh is the founder of Deendayal Research Institute, a voluntary Non-Governmental Organization (NGO) established in the year 1969. He is a social worker, reformer, original thinker and above all a man of action who dedicated his life to the service of motherland. His fieldwork, rural development and social reconstruction, started with Gonda experiment in the year 1978 which spread to other needy places in the country like Beed (Maharashtra) and Chitrakoot (M.P.). Shri Nanaji believed to the core that upliftment of the rural poor and strengthening the village life is the only solution for our country's progress. His precepts "Gramodaya" and "swavalamban" reflect the philosophy of the great personalities and Statesmen like Swami Vivekananda, Bal Gangadhar Tilak and Mahatma Gandhi. In him a great visionary and down to earth practical personality are blended together which is a rarity in nature. That is why, activities of all these centres were conceived and designed in minute details by Shri Nanaji. The success of these programmes is mainly due to the detailed planning and able execution under the constant guidance of Shri Nanaji. Several thousands of youth inspired by his personality and magnetized by his touch are participating in the programmes. The results achieved are always unique, astonishingly successful and even amazing some times.

All this was and is possible only because of radiant presence of Shri Nanaji. It is the legacy of Dr. Hedgewar, Shri M.S. Golwalkar (Guruji) and Pandit Deendayal Upadhyaya that is being carried out by Shri Nanaji in every thought and deed. True to this legacy Shri Nanaji believes that a nation or its constituent can never achieve an independent progress at the mercy of foreign funds. Shri Nanaji in spite of his several visits to foreign countries and easy accessibility to foreign funding agencies, never entertained the thought of raising money through these agencies. Time and again he stressed and is incessantly stressing this dictum. The resources required for every project, programme and endeavour of Deendayal Research Institute came from persons associated with or influenced by Deendayal Research Institute activities or from the Govt. of India. Thus, Deendayal Research Institute under the leadership of Shri Nanaji stands as a unique Non-Governmental Organization dedicated to the service of our motherland in its own unique way.

Sangh Parivar veteran and former Rajya Sabha member Nanaji Deshmukh passed away on 27 February, 2010 at the age of 94. He breathed his last at the premises of the country's first rural university he had established in this temple town bordering Madhya Pradesh and Uttar Pradesh, his close associate Sharda Prasad Dwivedi said, "Deshmukh was unwell for some time due to age-related ailments and had refused to be taken to Delhi for treatment". A Padma Vibhushan awardee, he had donated his body for medical research. Born in Kadoli in Maharashtra's Parbhani district on October 11, 1916, Deshmukh had founded Deendayal Research Institute here and was credited for exemplary work in the field of education, health and rural self-reliance. He was also instrumental in carrying out social restructuring programme in over 500 villages of both the states. Deshmukh had established the Chitrakoot Gramodaya Vishwavidyalaya in Chitrakoot—the country's first rural university—and was its Chancellor. Deshmukh was a key architect of Janata Party government that had broken the uninterrupted Congress-rule at the Centre in 1977. A man of the organization, Nanaji, as he was affectionately called by his friends and admirers, was a fighter who ended political untouchability of Bharatiya Jan Sangh, the erstwhile avatar of BJP, by giving total support to Jai Prakash Narayan's call for "Total Revolution" in 1974. The subsequent developments, including the Emergency imposed by Indira Gandhi, led to the formation of the Janata Party which stormed to power by sweeping off the Congress and Nanaji had played a prominent role in those dramatic moments. Nanaji's organizing skills during the JP Movement and the Emergency brought him an offer of the ministerial birth at the Centre in the Morarji Desai government but he declined. Nanaji had entered the Lok Sabha from Balrampur constituency in Uttar Pradesh in the election which saw Congress being wiped out of the state. He quietly told those concerned that his own inclination—and the way he saw his utility to the party—was in organizational work.

Earlier, in 1974 during the Bihar Sangharsh Movement, the selfless bachelor had saved JP from a police lathi-charge in Patna. In fact, at that time Nanaji left the swearing-in ceremony to Jagjivan Ram in an effort to persuade him how necessary his presence in the government was to ensure the stability of the new dispensation.

He was General Secretary of the Janata Party, along with socialist leader Madhu Limaye, but the new experiment was shortlived due to internal bickering and the controversy over dual membership. Nanaji left politics soon after he turned 60 though he was at the pinnacle of his career. He turned to social work to which he devoted himself till the end. Senior BJP leader V.K. Malhotra condoled the death of Nanaji Deshmukh. "He was a great visionary who will always be remembered for his devotion towards social causes", Malhotra said.

In a condolence message, Uttar Pradesh Chief Minister Mayawati said, during his long public life, Deshmukh served the people and played an important role to make weaker sections of the society self-reliant.

He would be remembered for his contribution towards the development of villages, she said.

Former Prime Minister Atal Bihari Vajpayee said Nanaji was

a dedicated social worker, lifelong pracharak of the RSS, senior politician and a visionary.

"He was an expert in handling challenges. There was a magnetic attraction in his personality and whoever came in touch with him remained with him throughout", Vajpayee said.

Recalling Deshmukh's role, Vajpayee said, "he was a fighter and joined the movement of Jai Prakash Narayan." His death is a loss to society and me personally," Vajpayee said in the condolence message.

Nanaji is a realistic spiritual embodiment of Indian giants and pioneers such as: Pandit Rama Bai, Madan Mohan Malviya, Jai Jawan Jai Kisan Lal Bahadur Shastri, Rabindranath Tagore, Sanjan Kasayi, Santh Kabir Das, Lokmanya Balgangadhar Tilak, Durga Bai Deshmukh, Lok Nayak Jaya Prakash Narayan and Mrs. Prabhavati and that of Sabarmati Experiment he put into action form of Chitrakoot experiment and now it became a living embodiment of human upliftment programme or *Deena Janoddarana.*

He is a Dadhichi by means of donating his body to the societal good.

...let us salute his spirit of freedom, self-worth, inherent dignity and human values and for promoting self-reliance in and among rural population through clarifying and clarion call of his Chitrakoot experiment, hence richly deserving to term his Birth Anniversary October 11 as National Day of Indian Professional SOCIAL WORK.

He is the rural India's modern sculpturer, an Indian Bruno CATALONO...and let it be the responsibility of Professional Social Work bodies, Schools of Social Work to incorporate his art and science of Social interventions and let NANAJI DESHMUKH waves weave novice textured quilted carpets of Professional Social Work Methods, modalities, and approaches of Community Organization, aimed at empowering, capacity building of individuals, groups through imbibing Nanaji Chitrakoot experiment. However, incomplete or complete, it remains as landmark art of Bruno CATALONO missing pieces of de Bruno CATALONO les Voyageurs.

It's now the turn of Professional Social Work in India to sleeve up its shirts and let's complement, supplement and implement NANAJI DESHMUKH modes of operationalization of installing and infusing self-reliance, resilience to face the challenges, and infusing the inherent self-worth and dignity of rural India by further incorporating NANAJI DESHMUKH'S thoughts and deeds into the flesh and blood of Professional Social Workers. Henceforth, NANAJI DESHMUKH becomes the reality of Maslowian fully functional personality and the self-actualized icon for Bhavya Bharathi's centuries to come. In fact, Nanaji would cease to be a person and he would be respected as a mark of the cultural renaissance in the stream of professional Social Work in India in specific and world at large and he fits to be an icon and a role model for *Bharatiyakaran* of Social Work profession or indigenization of Professional Social Work in India. He remains as an insignia of rural Social welfare and model of Welfare Economics and self-reliance and resilience and an ideological colossal for the prospective growth and development of Professional Social Work in India in the centuries to come...*he be remembered as Nalanda of Indian Social Work scenario who taught that there is unending happiness in giving our every minute but of indigenous interventions to Rural Self-reliance that makes India be alive and kicking up to Himalayan heights of progress and prosperity in the modern world in decades ahead.*

An Analysis on Nanaji: de Bruno Catalano les Voyageurs

On celebrating the Birth Anniversary of Nanaji Deshmukh *on 11th October, as National Day of Professional Social Work* on the contention that the contribution of Chitrakoot rural self-reliance model germinated as an independent experiment, does it fulfil the framework of professional Social Work? However, we need to recall the sculpture of Bruno Catalano of missing pieces, with many missing pieces too, still commands as a neo-world class art, in similar parlance, the initiatives of Nanaji could be the arguable variances with textual professional codes. However, Chitrakoot experiment remains as a masterpiece with whatever gaps ascribed in it by various professional echelons, as an initiative that filled many vacant stories of the human lives to the realized dreams to lead the self-reliant and vibrant lives with instilled self-worth and dignity as per the hard core professional elements of Social Work theory and practice. Thus, the spirited efforts of Nanaji in order to instill the self-worth, dignity and infusing self-reliance among the deprived and the marginalized rural population of India could be a one of its kind pioneering the Chitrakoot model of exercises in continuation of the pioneering Indian movements of community participation such as the Chipko movement, the Narmada Bachao Andolan, the Beti padao, the Silent Valley movement, and the Bhoodan Movement and the Dandi namak satyagraha movements along with the initiatives of Vandana Shiva and Baba Amte in the recent years.

We call the Dhruva tara that guides seafarers on to the right directions though it's not being textual it is highly contextual beyond all the modern machines fitted with GPS and advanced technologies. Thus, NANAJI DESHMUKH becomes Dhruva tara to the professional Social Work field, which may be with all gaps and differences in the hard core professional parameters being taught in the colleges of Social Work in India. The inputs of Chitrakoot do command the status of a North Star-Dhruva Tara that sets directions to the vessels in the oceans of professional social work for the centuries to come.

References

https://navbharattimes.indiatimes.com/state/uttar-pradesh/others/nanaji-deshmukh-awarded-with-bharat-ratna-here-is-all-about-his-life-and-works/amp_articleshow/70611185.cms

https://www.pmindia.gov.in/en/news_updates/pms-speech-at-the-birth-centenary-celebrations-of-nanaji-deshmukh-at-iari/?tag_term=nanaji-deshmukh&comment=disable

http://eprints.lincoln.ac.uk/id/eprint/14748/

https://www.researchgate.net/publication/324653979_Self_Help_India_Lessons_from_Bangladesh_and_Malaysia

https://m.economictimes.com/news/politics-and-nation/academics-question-proposal-to-observe-nanaji-deshmukhs-anniversary-as-social-work-day/articleshow/71530311.cms

https://en.m.wikipedia.org/wiki/Muhammad_Yunus

https://en.m.wikipedia.org/wiki/Nanaji_Deshmukh

www.chithrakoot.org

https://www.outlookindia.com/newswire/story/rss-veteran-nanaji-deshmukh-dead/675431

https://www.amazon.com/Jonathan-Livingston-Seagull-Richard-Bach/dp/0743278909

3
Social Work Practice
The Nanaji Way

Bishnu Mohan Dash

Introduction

India has a different social fibre which is incomparable to the European social thinking. What we have been doing as our duty and responsibility has become a profession in Europe. Social Work has been one such profession. It is high time that we understand the essence of Social Work from the Indian perspective. Nanaji Deshmukh has been one such social icon who taught us how to do selfless service to society. There is a need for documenting the experiments of Nanaji Deshmukh, to trace his social work models and practices and to incorporate his indigenous models which will definitely strengthen the social work education and Practice in India. Unfortunately, Nanaji Model of community development has not been included in the social work curriculum. The Bharatiya Samaj Karya Parishad, a national level association of social workers of India is engaged in popularizing the Nanaji model of community development which was subsequently added in the social work curriculum in many universities.

Need for Decolonizing Community Development Models

The contemporary social work is developed in reference to political power. The most of the models of community development and rural development taught to the students of social work are mostly Euro-American-centric. These models have not been tested for their adequacy and effectiveness. Ever since the introduction of social work courses in Indian universities since 1936, the reading lists in the subject of rural development/community development/community organization mostly written by foreign writers. The emphasis was always given to Western models of community development which is not relevant to Indian context. There has been a tendency to consider the Western models of community development as supreme and universal. The colonial mindsets to consider Europrean knowledge, paradigms as supreme still continue to be followed. The Indic models of community development have been completely sidelined. The focus had been to promote radical and Marxist approaches to social work. The successful models of community development particularly the initiatives of Nanaji Deshmukh, Baba Amte, Anna Hazare has been excluded in the social work curriculum. "Rothman's framework has been central to community organizing practice and pedagogy. However, the inattention to the centrality of culture in conceptualizing community organizing presents a key epistemological lacuna, which may challenge community practitioners' ability to develop the most appropriate community organizing strategies and interventions for the target milieu" (Laing, 2009). Hanna & Robinson (1994), Rothman (1995), and Checkoway (1995) have given various models of development. Since the introduction of first rural development programmes in Europe, the United States and other Western countries in the latter half of the 19th century, a great deal has been achieved but few would claim that the economic and social problems facing rural communities have been solved (Cazorla & Midgley, 2012). Still in India, many rural communities are deprived of various facilities and services. Despite the fact that Government of India and state governments have taken various initiatives and have implemented various community development programmes in addition to the contribution of various non-governmental organisations and civil society organizations. In this context, Nanaji's Chitrakoot model of development seems to be an important viable scheme to be replicated all over the rural areas of India to ensure sustainable community development.

The movement for *Bharatiyakaran* of social work education emphasizes on integrating the Indian indigenous models of rural development/community development in the social work curriculum. The European nature of social work professionalism and European nature of community development has been incorporated in the social work curriculum in Indian Universities. So, our social work professionals/rural development professionals find it difficult to apply these Western borrowed alien models in Indian context. The gap between theory and practice has widened and as a result our social work professionals are finding it difficult to relate these models to our social and cultural context. Though these Western models are not rooted in Indian culture, it has failed to develop cultural competence among social workers. The importance of culturally relevant interventions in order to remediate client problems have been highlighted in many studies (Lum, 2007; Weil, 1996). As Mao Tse-tung says, "Knowledge begins with practice, and theoretical knowledge, which is acquired through practice, must then return to practice."

Nanaji and Indian Social Work Day

In Nanaji model of development, he has placed greater emphasis on mobilizing people at the grassroots level and ensured their active participation in the development process. His model of development emphasized on community participation, integrated services for holistic development in the fields of education, health, agriculture, etc. He has developed a unique model of development relevant for the entire rural areas of India.

In this backdrop, the Indian models of community development assumes greater significance to enrich the practice skills of professional social workers in India. However, in India, working for society has been a result of one's own individual goodwill and noble intentions. Nanaji Deshmukh is an epitome of selfless work in the field of education, health and rural self-reliance and transformed many lives, that too, in some of the most backward villages of our country. Had it not been for his relentless efforts, these marginalized groups would have continued to languish in abject poverty, misery and deprivation. This silent crusader is a rare example, who chose social work over politics (Sehgal, 2019). He was one of the great champions for introducing his model of social reconstruction and community development. The primary objective of Nanaji Deshmukh's social work from Gonda to Chitrakoot was to create dedicated persons for society. This is because if such persons are created, the social work will be based on and supported by the society which would lead to the liberation of the entire society. It's very much relevant to commemorate Nanaji Deshmukh's birthday as the Indian Social Work Day because of he was a personality whose perspective for social work was in the tradition of Mahatma Gandhi, Vinoba Bhave and Deendayal" (Rajneesh Shukla, 2019).

"Bharat Ratna Nanaji Deshmukh institutionalized this concept of social service into professional social work" (Mukul Kanitkar, 2019). He further explained, "the traditional wisdom of *Sarve Bhavantu Sukhinah* (Let all be happy) exists as *Bahujan Hitaya Bahujan Sukhay* (Welfare of all, Happiness of all) which was defined as Sarvodaya by Mahatma Gandhi and Vinoba Bhave. Pandit Deendayal Upadhyaya gave a practical way of *Antyodaya* (Welfare of the last person) to achieve *Sarvodaya* (Welfare of All). Bharat Ratna Nanaji Deskhmukh institutionalized this concept into *Gramodaya* in which he created professional social workers. So the creation of a self-reliant society is an ideal to be achieved through unselfish social service, has to be institutionalized by way of professional social work. This is what Nanaji Deshmukh did from *Bharatiya* perspective in the modern time hence 11th October; his birthday should be celebrated as 'Bharatiya Samaj Karya Diwas'.

BSKP is a national level pan-India organization of social work professionals, academicians, researchers and students. In its 'Wardha Declaration' on 30th June, 2018, the BSKP unanimously adopted a proposal to observe 11th October, the birthday of Nanaji Deshmukh, as Indian Social Work Day or Bharatiya Samaj Karya Diwas. Since then the Indian Social Work Day is being celebrated in the Central as well as provincial social work institutions throughout the country. The request for declaration for Nanaji's birthday as Indian Social Work Day has been sent to Government of India for consideration. With his deep-seated commitment to the sustainable development of villagers and forest-dwellers defined by values of self-reliance, compassion and renunciation. He has given social work practice a new dimension which should be emulated in Indian Social Work curriculum." (Dash, 2019).

Bharat Ratna Chandikadas Amritrao Deshmukh (11th October, 1916 to 27th February, 2010), popularly called as Nanaji Deshmukh was also a sage of the kind who contextualized the ancient Indian knowledge and presented the holistic model of sustainable development in the field of village/rural development, tribal development, health, education, agro-forestry, animal husbandry, WASH (Water, Sanitation and Hygiene), public policy, field-work, community participation, advocacy, environment conservation, responsible consumption and production, life below water, life on earth and much more.

In his social work models and practice, Nanaji was inspired by the vision of integral humanism founded and propagated by his friend and ideological guide Deen Dayal (25th September, 1916 to 11th February, 1968). In fact, Nanaji was a true torch bearer of integral humanism and successfully implemented it in the field of social work. His social work models, field-work and practices all have imprints of integral humanism. The Chitrakoot Gramoday University, Madhya Pradesh and over 450 villages of India where he worked are eye witnesses to his contributions in social work from Indian perspective.

Sage of the Nation Nanaji Deshmukh: Architect of Integral Humanism

Birth	:	11th October 1916
Place	:	Kadoli in Hingoli district of Maharashtra
Parents	:	Rajabai (Mother), Amritrao Deshmukh (Father)
1934	:	Oath from Dr. Hedgewar to join Rashtriya Swayam-sevak Sangh
1940	:	A *Pracharak* in Gorakhpur, Uttar Pradesh
1948	:	First managing director of Swadesh Prakashan, Lucknow
1950	:	Establishment of India's first Saraswati Shishu Mandir in Gorakhpur
1951	:	Organising secretary of Bhartiya Jansangh (Uttar Pradesh)
1967	:	All India organising secretary of Bharatiya Jansangh

1968	:	Establishment of Deendayal Research Institute
1974	:	Sampoorn Kranti movement under leadership of Loknayak Jayprakash Narayan
1975	:	First general secretary of Lok Sangharsh Samiti for the anti-emergency rule, Imprison
1977	:	Bail, elected for Lok Sabha from Balrampur (Gonda), declined the portfolio of a minister, general secretary of ruling Janta Party
11 Oct., 1978	:	Retirement from politics, initiation of the constructive project
1978-1990	:	Constructive work in Gonda, Nagpur, Beed, Ahmedabad
1990-1991	:	Establishment of the first rural university in Chitrakoot, founder chancellor, Initiation of many socially useful projects, the inauguration of self-reliant mission in more than 500 villages of Chitrakoot area
11th Oct., 1997	:	Declaration to donate the body to All India Institute of Medical Sciences
1999	:	Padma Vibhushan and other awards, the award of honourary doctorate degree by Vadodara, Bundelkhand and Chitrakoot Universities
1999-2005	:	Nomination for Rajya Sabha by President of India
Death	:	27th February, 2010, Chitrakoot
Donation of the body	:	28th February, 2010, AIIMS, Delhi
2019	:	Bharat Ratna Award

Source: DEI, Delhi, 2020.

Social Work Practice: Nanaji Way

Nanaji's conviction was strong that the awakening and all-round development of people within the current political system is impossible. For this, on 20 April, 1978, he urged the politicians to dissociate themselves and come forward for constructive work but no one came. He was not disappointed. After delivering a historical speech in the presence of Jayaprakash Narayan in Patna on 8 October, 1978, he announced his retirement from active politics. He said that he would no longer contest elections and would spend his life in constructive work. At the age of 62, Nanaji built a big 54-acre campus and named it 'Jay Prabha Village', after Jayaprakash Narayan and his wife Prabhavati Devi. He decided on a mission statement, "water to every farm, work to every hand" and named four sources for the all-round development of rural life—self-reliance, education, health and harmony. For youths, he initiated 'Gramodaya' plan in Chitrakoot, so that they could get the education from primary to Masters in the village and could adopt village life instead of going to cities. He came to initiate a series of projects like *Arogyadham*, *Udyamita Vidyapeeth*, *Gopalan*, *Vanvasi Hostel*, *Gurukul*, etc.

With the construction of more than 27,000 tube-wells in Gonda district, he resolved the problem of farmers for irrigation and paved the way for its prosperity which was appreciated everywhere. Similarly, he worked in Beed for the establishment of *Gurukul* and in Nagpur for *Bal Jagat*. Around 1990-91, he came to be attracted to Lord Rama's workplace Chitrakoot and he decided to spend his remaining life there, by practising in different fields.

Gramodaya University in Chitrakoot was established by his inspiration and he was offered the post of Chancellor for it by the government which he accepted. But after the growing interference from the government, he resigned from it and started experimenting in different areas like education, health, morality and economic self-reliance. First introduced in 1950 and established in his leadership, Saraswati Shishu Mandir had expanded a lot by this time. Today, it has become a large non-governmental educational movement under the management of Vidya Bharti. Surendra Pal Gramoday Vidyalaya, Ramnath Ashram Shala, Parmanand Ashram Paddhati Vidyalaya, Nanhi Duniya, Entrepreneurship School, Cow Breeding Promotion and Research Centre, Ram Darshan and Arogyadham, as a foundation for the recovery of lifelong health, are attracting the attention of the whole country. Indian Council of Agricultural Research, influenced by the work of Nanaji has given Deendayal Research Institute the responsibility of operating four agricultural science centres in Gonda, Chitrakoot, Majhgaon and Beed. Apart from this, the Ministry of Human Resource Development has also given it the responsibility of operating three public educational institutes in Gonda, Chitrakoot, and Beed. There is hardly any prominent person in the educational, political or economic field, who had not the close affinity with Nanaji. He was accepted by all.

In recognition of his constructive work, the President of India nominated him for Rajya Sabha in 1999 so that the whole country gets the benefits of his work. He was also awarded Padmabhushan. On 7th February, 2010, Nanaji passed away leaving a large legacy.

To bring Pandit Deendayal Upadhyaya's philosophy of Integral Humanism to the practical level, Nanaji Deshmukh had established Deendayal Research Institute as a laboratory for socio-economic reconstruction. It was inaugurated by Guruji on 20 August, 1972 in Delhi. Deendayal Research Institute has presented many exemplary models of rural development and has successfully run it. This includes the projects on education, health, self-reliance, cow breeding and agricultural development.

Integral Humanism, as propounded by Pandit Deendayal Upadhyay, is such a concept of Indian philosophy that establishes the mutual compatibility of the relationship between man and society. This philosophy has the potential to make India a world leader by establishing India as a self-reliant country. The Deendayal Research Institute located in New Delhi is the centre for research and experiment which is working to fulfil this mission. The Gonda Gram Udaya Project started in Jaiprabha village in 1978, is a unique experiment in integrated rural development. Projects for social change were initiated with people's participation and initiative. Besides that, Nanaji has established various centres like Ramnath Arogyadham, Agricultural Science Centre, educational Institutes, hostels, for holistic and integrated development of villagers through measures like health care, providing quality education and agricultural development. Nanaji model for rural development is an excellent model of community development which should be replicated all over India to establish *Atmanirbhar* Bharat.

References

Carorla, A. and Midgley, J. (2012). Planning and Community Development: Case Studies, Grupo GESPLAN-UPM, Madrid (Spain), pp. 1-6.

Checkoway, B. (1995). "Six strategies of community change." *Community Development Journal*, 30 (1), 2-20.

Hanna, M. and Robinson, B. (1994). *Strategies for Community Empowerment*. Lewiston, NY: Edwin Mellen Press.

Laing, B.L. (2009). "A Critique of Rothman's and Other Standard Community Organizing Models: Toward Developing a Culturally Proficient Community Organizing Framework", *Community Development*, 40: 20–36.

Lum, D. (2007). *Culturally competent practice: A framework for understanding diverse groups*. (3rd ed.) Belmont, CA: Thompson Brooks Cole.

Rothman, J. (1995). "Approaches to Community Intervention", In Rothman, J., Erlich, J.L. and Tropman, J.E. (Eds.). *Strategies of Community Intervention*, Fifth Edition. Ithaca, Illinois: F.E. Peacock Publishers, Inc., pp. 26-63.

Sehgal, R. (2019). "Nanaji Deshmukh: A Champion of Rural Development", In *Social Work in India* (Eds.) Dash, B.M., Kumar, M. and Shukla, S., Concept Publishing Company (P) Ltd., New Delhi, pp. 1-12.

Weil, M. (1996). "Model development in community practice: an historical perspective." *Journal of Community Practice*, 4 (3-4).

4
Nanaji Deshmukh's Vision of Rural Development

Ranjana Sehgal

Social work education in India has, by and large, survived on foreign literature and information over the past 80 years, but Indian based scientific evidence is the need of the hour to enhance the effectiveness and credibility of the Social Work profession. At present, Indian social workers are dependent on the texts of foreign authors for practice direction. The lack of Indic content has rendered the profession deficient; hence it is imperative to create an indigenous knowledge base. A new approach for social work education in the *Bharatiya* context, one that capitalizes on the practice, relevant indigenous examples must be adopted. Our social work education should systematically produce lifelong learners, who appreciate the importance of Indic practice endeavours and who possess the skills necessary to identify, evaluate, and apply Indic perspective to their professional practice.

Bharatiya models of social work, that ought to have been an integral part of social work education and training, are rarely given their due recognition in our curriculum. History of Bharat is replete with indigenous models that have made immense contribution to the cause of social transformation of the weak and marginalised—Gandhian constructive work, Vinoba Bhave's *Bhoodan* and *Gramdaan*, Pt. Deen Dayal's Integral Humanism, Baba Amte's Anandwan—to name a few. These are exemplary social work experiments which have left indelible imprints on Indian soil. Here, it would be befitting to acknowledge the contribution of one of the most remarkable social worker of our times, who, albeit, had no formal degree of social work, but curated an innovative and sustainable model of social work practice, quite professional in its outlook. It is none other than the legendary Nanaji Deshmukh, popularly known as 'Yug-purush', who posthumously received the highest civilian award of our country, 'Bharat Ratna' in 2019. He singularly made outstanding contribution to the all-round development of some of the most backward areas of Bharat. The social work model sculpted by Nanaji, can fill the vacuum in Bharatiya Social Work Education, as our curriculum continues to remain impoverished for an indigenous knowledge and practice base.

From Politics to Social Work

At the peak of his political career, Nanaji turned down the ministerial post in the erstwhile government of Morarji Desai. He renounced public life for social work, as he realised, it was not possible to change society through politics. On his decision to suddenly quit politics, Nanaji had this to say, "it is an ultiduniya (upside down world) that we are creating. India's wealth, both in terms of people and natural resources, is in her villages. But the government is ignoring that. It is developing only cities and promoting consumerism". Disgusted with politicians, I decided to use young people to see what could be done in villages" (*India Today*, web desk New Delhi, 25 Jan., 2019).

Nanaji, recognised as the father of Indian coalition politics, was always inclined towards social work, and is today better known for his unique initiatives of eliminating poverty, improving rural health and creating institutions for rural education.

> "His equally, if not more relevant contribution was in developing a model of development, proven and tested... he is perhaps the only person in public life after Mahatma Gandhi for whom politics was not an end in itself, he made it meaningful, by testing development propositions in actual practice. He conclusively demonstrated the viability of Mahatma Gandhi's ideal of self-reliant village communities." *(Hazarika, March 2010).*

Nanaji Deshmukh was of the view that real change could not be engineered through political power and categorically stated, "I want to show that better work can be done without being in power", and true to his word, he actually made this possible through his unique social work model, which he curated for rural development. It is his social work experiments, which have earned him many accolades and have been largely instrumental in his posthumously getting the much coveted Bharat Ratna.

From *Gramodaya* to *Rashtrodaya*

According to Nanaji, the real India resided in its villages and not cities, and to develop the nation, the focus should be on the composite development of its villages. Nanaji's mission of meaningful rural development, 'from gramodaya to rashtrodaya' had its inception in Gonda (UP).

Jayaprabha gram Project of Nanaji is no longer in need of an introduction. Nanaji Deshmukh was elected to the Lok Sabha after defeating Rajmata Balrampur in 1977 from the Balrampur parliamentary seat. It is said that after losing the election, about 50 acres of Janaki Nagar Gram Panchayat was given by Rajmata as a donation to Nanaji. In order to bring Pandit Deendayal Upadhyaya's philosophy of Integral Humanism to a practice level, Nanaji Deshmukh established the Jayaprabha gram in Devipatan Mandal, as a laboratory for socio-economic reconstruction. Nanaji conceived the name Jayaprabha Gram by combining the first letters of the name of the couple Jayaprakash Narayan, and his wife Prabhadevi. He was a great admirer of Jaya Prakash Narayan and when JP along with his wife Prabhavati started 'Samagra Kranti', greatly impressed by their work, he joined as General Secretary in the revolutionary movement.

Development of villages, based on Pt. Deendayal Upadhyaya's philosophy of 'Integral Humanism, which would make the villages self-sufficient and independent of government hand-outs, became the mission of Nanaji. He did not believe in charity but social reform, as in charity you give, in social reform you empower. No wonder that Nanaji is today acclaimed as a great reformer of 20th century, who worked in such backward areas, where no one ever dared to go and work. After successfully working in backward areas of Gonda, and Beed, he finally decided to make Chitrakoot, the *karambhoomi* of Vanwasi Ram as his 'prayogshala'. Through his experiments in Chitrakoot, he presented an indigenous model of constructive rural reconstruction, encapsulating his vision of what rural India should be like, and transformed it into a unique and successful model. The Chitrakoot model, as it is popularly known, is about integral humanism, holistic and inclusive development, which made rural development as the basis of national development, whose impact spread not only in the state but in the whole country.

Deendayal Research Institute (DRI)

In 1972 to validate and propagate the philosophy of integral humanism propounded by Pandit Deendayal Upadhyaya (1916–1968), Nanaji founded the Deendayal Research Institute (DRI). After abdicating politics in 1980, Nanaji turned to full time social work through the Deendayal Research Institute (DRI), which became the fulcrum of his social work model. "After the untimely death of Pt. Deendayal Upadhyaya in 1968, Nanaji established the Deendayal Research Institute in Delhi, to push the unfinished works of Deendayalji. It became a role model for rural and social development and encouraged a number of youth to join social work". (Deb, 2019)

The mission statement of Deendayal Research Institute goes as follows, "We are not for ourselves but our kith and kin; our kith and kin are those who are oppressed and neglected."

The aim of the Institute has been to evolve a social system for the transformation of our age-old Indian society to the modern scientific era, but based on eternal values of integral Humanism. With this aim, Deendayal Research Institute, which was the brain-child of Nanaji is even today in the forefront, carrying out various programmes with the following objectives:

- To carry out research in Social Science with a view to reconstruct Indian Society.
- To establish Rural Development and Training centres for carrying out research with a view to motivate people in adopting new and improved technologies in the field of sustainable Agriculture, Water Conservation & Alternative Industrialization and promote self-employment.
- Activities in the field of medical research, medical care, life-long health and medical education.
- To set up Academic and Technical Vocational Training centres in rural areas.
- To eradicate social evils by propagating human values with the active cooperation and initiative of the people.
- To establish a dispute free Society.
- To promote Integrated Tribal Development.
- To ensure people initiative and active participation in the efforts.
- To organize Intellectual Activities.
- To share the experience and Intellectual property with other Organizations (www.chitrakoot.org)

Nanaji also established the Chitrakoot Gramodaya Vishwavidyalya, India's first ever rural university, his gift to India. (Jan 26, 2019 News18.com) He developed many successful modules of skill development, character building, employment generation, water conservation, health and hygiene, self-help and poverty alleviation, which are lessons on sustainable and integrated rural development waiting to be replicated in rest of the country.

Integrated Child Development

Nanaji was a visionary, who put great emphasis on integrated development of the child, an educationist, who understood the value of school education, but was unhappy, that the government had not done enough in this regard, *"Education is what makes students responsible towards society. Therefore, without any discrimination, equal education should be provided to every child and girl in the society. The overall development of the nation and the health of society depends on equal education for all. Unfortunately, contrary work is being done in independent India."* (*Virat Purush*, vol. 2)

He established India's first Shishu Mandir at Gorakhpur in 1950. It was an outcome of his love for education and in response to the threat he perceived after Independence, from the missionary schools, to the society in general and indigenous education system in particular. At that time there was no such organized effort either on the part of the government or the civil society to counter this threat.

> "In 1947 he was sent to Gorakhpur in UP as RSS pracharak, where he established a Saraswati Shishu Mandir in 1950. It was the first school of the present day Saraswati Shishu Mandir education system, having numerous schools in its fold all over the country. Saraswati Shishu Mandir was the result of Nanaji's vision towards child education and its role in human's all-round development—manav ka sampoorna vikas". (Deb, Feb., 2019).

Revival of *Gurukul* System

The *Gurukul* has been our ancient education and learning system that existed since the Vedic age. The students lived in *ashrams* and were treated as a part of *Guru's* family. Apart from education, the *Gurus* trained their students in meditation, *yoga* and taught Vedas, based on the tradition known as *Guru-shishya* tradition. The students were treated equally, irrespective of their social standards. The *gurukul* system was the only education system known at the time. The students gained in-depth knowledge, and were taught essential aspects for a cultured and disciplined life. The *Shishyas* lived under the *gurukul* roof with a spirit of brotherhood, and love.

Nanaji's vision of the 'ancient Indian idyll' transported to the modern age, cannot be complete without discussing his efforts of the revival of the concept of *Gurukul* in Chitrakoot. He established schools that followed the ancient Indian *Gurukul* system. 'There is the Surendra Paul School in Chitrakoot, named after the late younger brother of NRI industrialist Swaraj Paul; and the Ramnath Ashram, again in memory of Goenka, for 200 live-in *adivasi* (tribal) students. At the spanking-clean and efficiently run Ramnath Ashram, the day begins with prayers followed by *yoga*. (Saba Naqvi Bhaumik, *India Today*, August 11, 1997). The main focus of the *Gurukul* system was, a character development, personality development, intellectual development, spiritual development, and preservation of *Bharatiya* knowledge and culture.

The *Gurukul* was a comprehensive learning centre, where the students were taught good habits of respecting the mother, father, elders and the teachers. On the whole, the ancient system gained a huge respect with Nanaji's *Gurukulam* system, where he developed this unique system where, he invited retired old couples from across the country, and entrusted them with full care and all-round development of the students of *Gurukul*. They were called *Gurumata* and *Gurupita* and one couple was responsible for the care of 20-25 children, giving love and care like grandparents. This unique model of Nanaji was in sync with the Indian culture and tradition, hence better suited to our social context, as against the foster care model, popular in the West.

Samaj-Shilpi Dampati: Sculptors of Society

Nanaji's contribution to rural reconstruction is unprecedented, and his innovative interventions, were akin to the professional social worker's role as conceived in the West, but with a difference. He created a novel and noble concept of 'Samaj-shilpi Dampati', sculptors of society—the focal point for implementation of all his developmental work, activities and programmes at DRI. On an analysis of the role of 'Samaj shilpi Dampati', one cannot but see the similarities between the role of the *dampati* and that of a trained social worker. This *dampati* lived in the villages and helped the villagers access health and educational facilities and all the government schemes. Self-reliance and empowerment which also happen to be the integral goals of professional social work were the basic premise of their interventions. They documented all their activities and acted as enablers and facilitators for the villagers. The data so generated is a valuable source for policy and planning of rural development programmes in India. The novel idea of keeping the husband-wife together in rural development programmes was indeed a unique one, as it helped them maintain a work life balance with a deep sense of commitment, involvement and participation at the grassroot level.

Initially, it was a big challenge for these young men and women to enlist the participation of the villagers for developmental and creative work, but this was soon made possible under the dynamic leadership of Nanaji, as a part of his *swamlamban abhiyaan*. Each 'Samaj shilpi Dampati', was responsible for a cluster of 2-5 villages, to which they committed to give 5 years of their lives with a goal of uplifting them by making them self-reliant with the available resources. An important component of self-reliance was that a nominal fee was charged for every service rendered, so as to make every centre self-sustaining. Enlisting the participation of the villagers and motivating those divided by caste and politics, towards constructive work was a difficult and challenging task, but in no time these 'Samaj shilpi Dampati', won the hearts of the villagers through their selfless work and became part of their families. Once unfamiliarity turned into close family like ties, began the journey of development of that village. This approach is the same as embodied in social work principles of relationship and acceptance put into actual practice.

The Way Forward for Social Worker Educators

Nanaji was highly pained to see how the policy-makers had completely neglected the rural population, at best considering them fit only for subsidies and hand-outs, rather than empowering them, consequently subjecting them to a life of dependency. Leading by example, he proved in a short span, how the villages could be developed and made self-reliant by putting systems in place, more as a corporate practice, than piecemeal approach, where individuals are at their efficient best, something rare among NGOs. Nanaji's contribution to rural reconstruction is particularly significant, as it did not entail use of any extra resources but operated within the existing government schemes. His model of social work in fact can well be developed as a case study to demonstrate optimal use of the available governmental schemes and development initiatives can be made for creating a viable and self-reliant rural India.

Nanaji's sustainable development model is particularly important and relevant to the movement of *Bhartiyakaran* of professional social work. Social work education should appreciate the importance of Indic practice endeavours and produce learners who possess the skills necessary to identify, evaluate, and apply Indic perspectives to their professional practice. Unfortunately, the art and science of social work is still not applied in its true spirit in our country, posing a serious threat to its very survival. Unless modified and adapted to our socio-cultural context, for all intent and purposes, professional social work may well become a 'business enterprise in human relationships'. Comprehensive discussions on *Bharatiya* social work experiments will enable a fresh appreciation of our rich glorious history, and help us understand the subtle similarities and differences in the Indian and Western approach and perspective of social work.

It goes without saying that practical experience in varied social work settings is the best medium for a student to develop his understanding and skills of dealing with psycho-social problems. The model of Nanaji has been a subject of research and investigation for many a scholars from abroad and India, but unfortunately, our students have rarely been systematically exposed to recently developed methods for identifying, critically appraising, and integrating, relevant research findings into their practice activities on a real-time basis. His contribution to rural reconstruction is unprecedented and has no parallel, hence needs an in-depth study by social work research scholars as a basis for developing indigenous innovative social work approaches and intervention strategies. He was a true champion of the rights of the weak and poor, especially of the rural and backward Bharat and it is our proud privilege to have his body of work, to draw inspiration from.

References

"Nanaji Deshmukh: Harbinger of Indian Culture", *Uday India*, Nov. 4, 2016.

India Today, web desk New Delhi 25 Jan 2019, Who is Bharat Ratna Nanaji Deshmukh? Key things to know about him.

Dharmendra Deb, Feb. 2019, www.barakbulletin.com

Ankur Sharma, Oct. 11, 2017, hindi, one India.

Upmanyu Hazarika, www.outlook.com website

Virat Purush, (Vol. 2) 2014, Deendayal Shodh Sansthan, Prabhat Prakashan, New Delhi.

Saba Naqvi Bhaumik, *India Today*, August 11, 1997.

5
Integral Humanism as the Guiding Principle of Social Work

Mithilesh Kumar and *Rajan Prakash*

Historical Background

'Integral Humanism' originated as a link in the series of historical thought process. It was the result of the combination of ancient Greek and European Renaissance of the 16th century and the Indian Renaissance of the 20th century. The divine monarchy, i.e. the Roman Empire based on the principle of theocracy was challenged in Greece and subsequently 'Humanism' came into existence, in the light of ancient Greek philosophy against 'God' and 'mysticism'. In the mid-15th century, after the fall of Constantinople, the character of the equatorial civilisation changed. This period in world history is termed as the period of exploration and conquest of the earth. With the rise of new technology in ship making and navigation Columbus came to discover the 'new world'. Copernicus, Galileo and Newton's scientific endeavours in research changed the direction and vision of thinking. This period witnessed the replacement of invisible divine power by conscience, discussion, courage and the scientific and sociological study of matter and its forms became more prominent.

What many scholars consider the Renaissance—the result of the new thought process of the human mind—and exaggerate its achievement, the European Imperialism defied it with its plundering nature of wealth and other civilizations. It sought to enslave humanity with its superior development in the field of science and technology. This European enslavement of another world, the pain inflicted by its imperialism, and in the self-respect grew the Asian Renaissance led by India. Raja Rammohun Roy, Swami Vivekananda and Dayanand Saraswati came to play the pioneering role in reordering their society to protect it from foreign intrusion. One key figure in India of the 20th century who introduced the world with the spiritual possession of India was Swami Vivekananda who has a great zeal and enthusiasm for Indian culture[1]. When the west tried to look upon the east as inferior, Vivekananda expressed his opinion:

> "In America, I found them to be full of *rajo-guna*. They will now try to proceed to *sattva-guna*. All Europe is predominantly active in achieving material success, but America leads them all in this respect. Bharata was *sattva-pradhana* during the days of *rishis*. Even now inside the bone and marrow, India is still *sattva-guni*. Among all the nations of the world, Bharata is still *sattvika* — more so than anyone else — but on the outer shell, it has become full of *tamas*. For a long time, they have been passing through a great storm, and their bad days have not ended yet. It is the hunger that is killing the nation, and the whole race is dying out slowly. Our duty is to give them food and education."[2]

From Raja Rammohun Roy to Deendayal Upadhyay, the period of about eighty years was of the constant struggle between Western and Indian thought, worldview knowledge and practice. At the core of the Western ethnocentrism was the intent to take away the material wealth of the other civilization as a reaction to which many people and worldview emerged. One such worldview is the 'Integral humanism' which represents the thought and ideas of a great philosopher Pandit Deendayal Upadhyay who wanted to retain the identity of Bharata but not to isolate the rest of the world, who wanted to make it modern but not the imitation of the West, who wanted to touch the pinnacle of science and knowledge but not at the cost of rejecting spirituality. There are two aspects of 'Integral Humanism,' first is the Western philosophy and the second, Indian culture. 'Humanism' is primarily the Western idea whereas the 'integration' is Indian. Thus, 'Integral humanism' is the result of *Bhartiyakaran* of *manavvad.* It is not the view of struggle but of synthesis.

Everything that was prevalent in the West was not acceptable even by its own people. Hence, the change became inevitable, which came in the form of the renaissance. European renaissance resisted the earlier prevalent life. The dignity of human against the divine power, secular state in the place of religious universalism, human courage against the divine mercy, conscience instead of mystical truth and research against the established values are the bases of European renaissance. The religious superstition of the Western world had made the spiritual bottom of humans so mystic, divine dependent and hypocritical that they became orthodox and materialistic. While Deendayal was not against Western life, he was cautious of its deformation. He believed that people fascinated by the West ignored its ills, and were trying to make India an imitation of the West. This situation, according to him, created an illusion in the society. He wrote:

> "After the Gandhiji passed away, those who were entrusted with the power of the state, could not understand the language and spirit of India nor could they realise their dream. We saw our whole life and problem through the lens of the West. Consequently, West has a deep mark on our politics, economics, society, literature and culture. Different political parties, either socialist or not, are trying to echo the west."[3]

This is why Deendayal was against the blind imitation of the Western world at the same time he respected all human efforts. He also wanted to adopt those ideas which were in the interest of the human. The analysis of the Western world by Deendayal is in line with the Gandhian thought and it sought to propose an alternative national model for Jawaharlal Nehru's 'Democratic Socialism' which was influenced by the Western ideals.

Indian Culture

There is an eternal continuity in the Indian Culture. Despite several dark areas India is unbound economically, politically and socially and possess the power to be the leader of the world. Shri Aurobindo wrote for India,

> "There is no country in the world who has revealed an immense power, even after being suppressed for so long under an alien rule. This moral strength, this capacity to reach the root and whole right over its own self — these are the secrets of the power of Asia. Our holy books have told us that those who could rule over himself can rule all over the world. *Swaraj* could only become the Samrat."[4]

In the metaphysical aspect, Deendayal's view is not opposed to that of Shri Aurobindo but he differs from him on the aspect of Maurya and Gupta empire. Deendayal is one who considers 'Gupta Empire' the 'golden age' of India but this is his reactionary approach as foreign powers were intruding into the politically-independent culture of India. Thus, he holds affection for Shankaracharya and Kautilya who attempted to unite India culturally and politically respectively. He focused more on the positive aspects of Indian culture and attributed all these to it while for the negative aspects he holds human nature, external and foreign contact responsible. Thus, India holds supreme value in his thought but this does not mean that he justified status quo at the cost of cultural supremacy.

Evolution of the Nomenclature

The roots of the nomenclature of the 'Integral Humanism' is in the concept of '*shuddha rashtravad*' adopted by Rashtriya Swayamsevak Sangha. Rashtriya Swayamsevak Sangh believed that Indian culture is essential 'Hindu Culture' and idea of independent India should be based on this ideal. It was the result of Indianness and also grew as a result of the reaction to mixed nationalism adopted by Congress which was heavily Western.

In the first session of Jan Sangh held in December 1952, Deendayal put forth the resolution relating to the cultural revivalism. It was a 'Hindu Nationalist' resolution and in 1953 he proposed the economic framework of Jan Sangh in the regional meet of Uttar Pradesh. In 1958 at the annual session of Jan Sangh, the idea of both capitalism and socialism were openly and heavily criticised and Jan Sangh termed these as foreign thought for centralisation of power. It reiterated its resolution for decentralisation of power and cultural revivalism. It was said that socialism and capitalism alike are the thought of centralisation of power whereas Jan Sangh always stood for its decentralisation. While delivering a lecture on it, Pandit Deendayal Upadhyay first presented the aspect of 'humanism' against the ideas of capitalism and socialism on 11 March, 1959 in Lucknow in Gangaprasad Memorial Hall. He used the word 'humanism' for the first time in this speech which was against the prevalent mechanistic view of society. In the session of Jan Sangh from 11 August to 15 August, 1964 held in Gwalior, Upadhyay presented the document titled 'Principle and Policy' and 'integral humanism' was the name given to represent the ideas of the party. From 22-25 April, 1965, Upadhyay kept on describing this view in the conference organised by the Jan Sangh in Bombay. With the assassination on 11 February, 1968 under mysterious condition while travelling in train the work on the expansion of this idea also came to a halt.

Apart from 'integral humanism' Upadhyay's colleagues used to call this worldview by different names like 'ekatmvad', 'samanavit manawvad', 'paripurn manawvad' etc. A number of scholars argue that 'ism' or 'vaad' is not in Indian tradition and '*Dharma*' and 'Darshana' are used in the place of 'ideology'. There is a great emphasis on 'Manav Dharma' not on *Manawvad* in Indian scriptures. The natural question may arise that why did Upadhyay choose to term in 'ism'. According to Dattopant Thengadi 'humanism' was chosen for the sake of layman, as everyone is used to having a fixed framework of observation and thinking.[5] In fact, what Upadhyay meant was not an ideology with a fixed lens of observation rather he conceptualised it as an integral philosophy of the entire system which is the essence of Indian culture and tradition. The Western civilisation first presented the human as against the god and later describes him mechanically. Upadhyay presented the human neither against the god nor as a mechanical entity rather as a complete entity.

As a Worldview

The subject of examination of 'integral humanism' is the humans and their relationship with the community. Dattopant Thengadi argues that every entity, institution and concept in the West is viewed as compartmentalised. Human is viewed as intact from human, family independent of family and society with no relation with society. In this conceptualisation, the relationship between these units is ignored.[6]

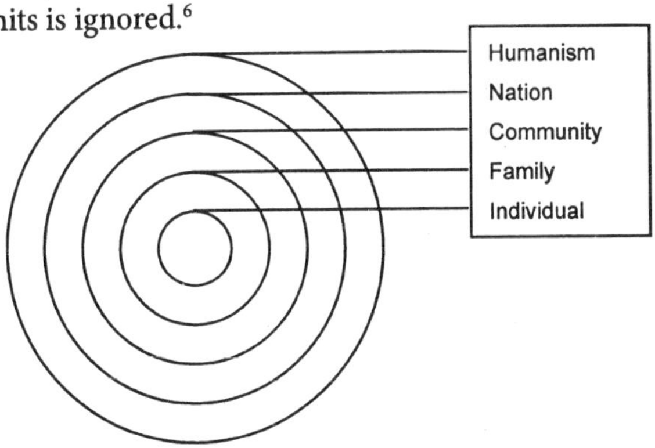

Fig. 5.1: Five concentric circles representing the different units

This can be depicted through **Fig. 5.1**. In this figure, the human is at the centre who is encircled by the family which in turn is encircled by the community, nation and the entire humanity. This depiction is concentric and each circle prevents the relation of the inner from the outer. Although the constituent entity is encircled, in fact, no entity is connected with the others. Contrary to this belief the thought process in Indian tradition is spiral or cyclic. It is eternal and this is why we call it '*Sanatana*'. The spiral depiction of the world in our thought process does not break the contact of one from another, but it connects each other. Our thought process conceptualises, the first coil of the spiral as an individual, the second as family, the third as a community, the fourth as a nation and so like the infinite end with the whole humanity at the end. Thus, there is no breakage in this system and it also signifies that humanity is connected with all the entities.

Abandoned Mission of Social Work and the Need for Humanism

Social work or any other humanitarian discipline for that matter grew out of the concern for the human, to make their life easy and in harmony with the society. In the West, the rapid industrialisation and rise of the urban poor gave birth to a scientific discipline aimed to provide a solution for the individual problems without creating dysfunction in society. However, in the long journey of its mission, it has abandoned its very mission. Today professionals view individual responsible for the societal problem and society for the individual discontent. When the discipline of social work has hardly overcome its 'justification dispute'[7], it is alarming to see the recent trend of promoting the individualistic solution to the problems, alienated from the family, friends, community and the civic involvement which were for long the traditional system of meaning and fulfilment. The individualistic approach might work in the favour of the individual but it certainly alienates the family, community and society and at times makes them uncomfortable.

Today the profession has reduced itself to the 'therapy' providing service for every problem. The scenario in the West is that one will find social workers frequently engaged in psychotherapy and counselling service but very few are providing services to old age, family and community and society. It is true that the social workers encounter frequent cases of anxiety, depression, mental trauma and those relating with the psychological state of mind of the individual. There is nothing wrong in teaching the professionals about these ailments and practising for it, but a large number of social workers leaving the social service and its content finding little place in social work curriculum is beyond justification. The world-view of individual and society against and incompatible to each other is not compatible with the functional world-view of society which sees the function of every entity in everything. Overly obsessed with the economic determinism, the social work has increasingly come to reduce the individual as an economic entity. Thus, it is no surprise that the cultural importance is being neglected. However, the failure of the profession to incorporate the holistic approach of well-being is increasingly being seen as the failure of the discipline as a whole. Prof. Hary Specht and Mark Courtney have examined the fall of the profession in their work—'Unfaithful Angels: How Social Work Has Abandoned its Mission.'[8] This work is an important milestone in that it challenges the universally held belief of the American Model of Social Work as an intrinsically individualistic and appropriate with the society of America. Prof. Hary Specht and Courtney show that no society is intrinsically individualistic and the imposition of individualist solution to the societal or even individual problems is very much responsible for the fall of the profession from its original mission of service to just a therapy giving enterprise.

When we are much obsessed with the replication of the Americal Model of Social Work, Prof. Specht shows the very essential 'qualities' of that profession in American society. There is a much pervasive misconception even in the academic community of social work that professionalism means the abandonment of the charity and social service. This emanates from the belief that the adoption of a scientific approach necessarily demands the replacement of the previous approach of working with the people by a new 'scientific approach'. This has led to the imitation of the Western model of the profession in the Third World countries ignoring the fact that each and every society has differences in it and it can be disastrous to impose the value of one on the other.

The profession of social work has the ultimate goal of universal empowerment and functionalism, i.e. making every entity functional with each other, not against each other. The old mission of social work is not to make one alienated from the other but nurturing everyone in harmony. We cannot think of developing the individual, disconnected from family, community and society, as each one is related to the other and there is an element of integration in it. This is the basic principle of integral humanism. The term is relatively new but the value is eternal. Social work is a profession with the aspect of working with the people and we cannot dissociate the moral aspect from it.[9] Upon closely analysing the social work, we find that integral humanism must be its basic value and guiding principle in the field as well as in education. Deendayal Upadhyay's work in bringing out a perspective with its root in Indian scriptures can be applied to the social work not only in India but abroad as well, as it makes no distinction between East or West and also gives due weightage to the local circumstances not because of the ethnocentricism but because of the practical reasons. In a time when social work is using compartmentalised worldview of the system, integral humanism offers the path of universal humanism and brings out harmony and functionalism in the society. If the Social Work has to strengthen its root in the academic world this must be included in the curriculum with a broad emphasis on the perspective explained by Deendayal. Nanaji Deshmukh experimented with this worldview in Gonda and Chitrakoot and showed that it is not only theoretical but can be applied in the field too. New professionals can connect with the local examples more than that of unknown and alien society having no relevance in Indian society. This will also help the profession to get back its mission with a humanitarian nature of service, with the creation of self-reliant, self-sustained, self-fulfilling society.

Notes

1. Chakraborty, S.K. (2016). *Swami Vivekananda: Leader of Sacred Nationhood*. Advaita Ashrama (A publication branch of Ramakrishna Math, Belur Math).
2. *Reminiscences of Swami Vivekananda* (n.d.). Retrieved from https://www.ramakrishnavivekananda.info/reminiscences/339_mng.htm.
3. Translated by the authors from, Upadhyay, D. (nd). *Swatantrata ke Sadhan aur Siddhi*. Unpublished manuscript.
4. Quoted from T. Preeti (2017). *Architect of A Philosophi: Deendayal Upadhyay*. New Delhi: Bhartiya Sahitya Sangrah.
5. Upadhyaya, D., & Thengadi, D.B. (1979). *The Integral Approach*. Deen Dayal Research Institute.
6. *Ibid.*
7. Abbot, Andrew (1988). *The System of Professions*. Chicago: University of Chicago Press.

8. Specht, H., & Courtney, M.E. (1995). *Unfaithful angels: How social work has abandoned its mission.* Simon and Schuster.
9. Bisman, C. (2004). "Social work values: The moral core of the profession." *The British Journal of Social Work*, 34(1), 109-123.

References

Abbot, A. (1988). *The System of Professions.* Chicago: University of Chicago.

Bisman, C. (2004). "Social work values: The moral core of the profession." *The British Journal of Social Work*, 34(1), 109-123.

Chakraborty, S.K. (2016). *Swami Vivekananda: Leader of Sacred Nationhood.* Advaita Ashrama (A publication branch of Ramakrishna Math, Belur Math). Press.

Reminiscences of Swami Vivekananda (n.d.). Retrieved from https://www.ramakrishnavivekananda.info/reminiscences/339_mng.htm.

Specht, H., & Courtney, M.E. (1995). *Unfaithful angels: How social work has abandoned its mission.* Simon and Schuster.

Upadhyay, D. (nd). *Swatantrata ke Sadhan aur Siddhi.* Unpublished manuscript.

Upadhyaya, D., & Thengadi, D.B. (1979). *The Integral Approach.* Deendayal Research Institute.

6
Chitrakoot Model of Sustainable Village Development

Charu Sethi

Introduction

> "Sustainable development is the pathway to the future we want for all. It offers a framework to generate economic growth, achieve social justice, exercise environmental stewardship and strengthen governance."
>
> —*Ban Ki-Moon*

Sustainable Development is an important approach to development, which affects everyone. The impact of the decision of the society holds real consequences on the lives of people. Sustainable development provides an approach to make better decisions on the issues that affect the lives. It is about finding a better way of doing things which benefits present and future generations. The modern concept of sustainable development was derived in year 1987 from the Brundtland Report, which was rooted in sustainable forest management. As the concept developed, it has shifted its focus more towards the economic development, social progress and environmental protection for the future generations. It is suggested 'sustainability' should be seen as the goal of human-ecosystem equilibrium, while 'sustainable development' refers to the holistic approach. In holistic approach, sustainable community takes into account, multiple human needs. It is a place where people of diverse backgrounds and perspectives feel safe, where all the groups of people have a say in decision-making and the prosperity is shared. A sustainable community manages its human, natural, and financial capital to meet current needs while ensuring that adequate resources are available for the future generations. Sustainable development is meeting the goals of human development while simultaneously sustaining the ability of natural resources upon which the economy and society depends. The focus of sustainable development is broader than just the environment. It is also about ensuring the strong, healthy and just society. Sustainable development means meeting the diverse needs of all the people in the present as well as future while promoting personal well-being, social cohesion and creating equal opportunities. United Nations Member States (2015) adopted 17 Goals of Sustainable Development, known as Global Goals. They all call for the action to end poverty, protect the planet and ensure that all the people enjoy peace and prosperity by 2030. These 17 goals are integrated— that is they recognize that the action in one area will affect outcomes in others and the development must balance social, economic and environmental sustainability.

Background of the Sustainable Development

In 1992, at Rio de Janerio, the concept of Sustainable Development was raised in the United Nations Conference on Environment and Development. It was the first international attempt to draw up action plans and strategies for moving towards a more sustainable pattern of development. It was attended by all the Heads of the countries and National governments. Sustainable development was the solution to the problems of environmental degradation as discussed by the Brundtland Commission in the 1987 report—"Our Common Future".

In 2002, at Johannesburg, the World Summit on Sustainable Development was held which delivered three key outcomes: a political declaration, the plan of implementation and a range of partnership initiatives.

The key features of Sustainable Development are:

- Technological development shall be input effective and not input utilizing.
- The rate of consumption should not surpass the rate of salvation.

- For renewable resources, the rate of consumption should not surpass the rate of production of renewable substitutes.
- All types of pollution should be minimized.
- Sensible use of natural resources.

The goals of Sustainable Development are:

- To promote the development through minimizing the environmental problems.
- To meet the needs of the existing generation without compromising the quality of the environment for the future generations.

Sustainable Development and COVID-19

The COVID-19 (corona virus) pandemic is the global health crisis. Since its emergence in Asia (China), the virus has spread voraciously everywhere in the world. All the nations are in a race to slow down the spread of the virus by testing and treating patients, carrying out contact tracing, limiting travel, quarantining citizens, and cancelling large gatherings such as sporting events, concerts, and educational institutions. But, COVID-19 is much more than a health crisis. It has the potential to create devastating social, economic and political crises that will leave deep scars on the development of each nation. Health is a fundamental human right and the foundation of economic prosperity and security. This global crisis is a sharp reminder that everyone, everywhere should have access to qualitative, affordable and sustainable health services.

The report by the United Nations Development Programme suggests all nations to ensure that their actions against Corona should be comprehensive as well as equitable and inclusive, so that no one is left out and country can continue to make progress in achieving the Sustainable Development Goals. In these lines, all the countries must also consider ways to prevent a similar pandemic recurring. People and nature must be at the centre of this deep transformation for redistribution, regeneration and restoration. Prosperity for people and the planet is possible only if we take right decisions today, so that future generations can survive and thrive in a better world. The Corona virus pandemic is more than a health crisis. It is rooted in how we treat our planet, how we prioritize our public spendings (UNDP, 2020).

The concept of sustainable development also encompasses *the Sustainable village development* which is vital to the economic, social and environmental viability of the country. It is essential for poverty eradication in rural areas. The manifestation of poverty has transcended the urban-rural divide—it has sub-regional and regional contexts. Village development initiatives contribute to sustainable livelihoods through efforts at the global, regional, national and local levels.

Sustainable Village Development

> "Sustainable village means a place that is totally committed to provide a better life quality for its inhabitants. It is a village that has all the necessary conditions to live in community, respecting the environment, traditions, education, respecting the people and its values, and where every person is really involved in the local improvement of the social aspects. Share the ideas and solve the problems in a community basis, because everyone is focused in 'doing their best' to the sustainability of their village/community."
>
> — *Cristina M.*

The sustainable village development addresses multiple human needs. It manages its human, natural, and financial capital to meet current needs while ensuring that adequate resources are available for future needs and generation. It is a place where all the people of diverse backgrounds and perspective feel socially safe, economically equitable with viable environment. Sustainable Village Development is a long-term perspective, focusing on adapting to change in both the present and future (*see* Fig. 6.1).

In our country, two-third of the people live in villages. Their average income is only about half of the average income of their

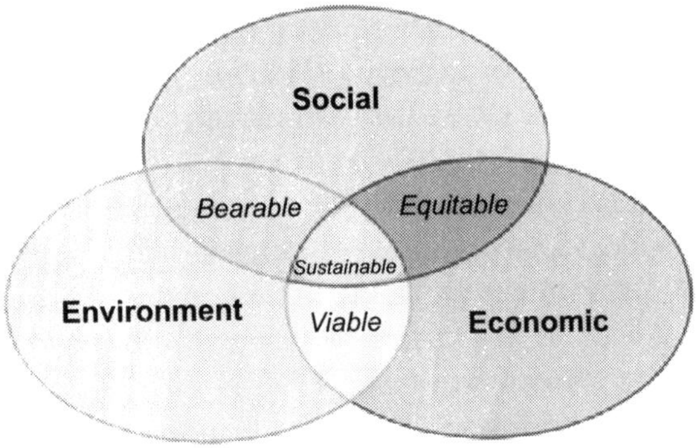

Fig. 6.1: Sustainable Development should be socially, economically and environmentally sustainable.

urban counterparts. Creating conditions to raise their income is still a challenge. Knowledge-based technologies allow income generation activities in the village area. On the contrary, people in village depends upon local geographical conditions for agriculture and small scale industrial activities. The village economy is volatile to natural hazards like—floods, landslides, drought and poor agricultural productivity. The other challenges faced by rural areas such as climate change, deforestation, land degradation, fragmentation of natural habitat, loss of biodiversity, poverty and social isolation. People are prone to extreme poverty, famine, social exclusion and environmental injustice.

A healthy and dynamic agricultural sector is an important foundation, or we can say a crux for village development. Rural livelihoods are enhanced through effective participation of rural people and rural communities in the management of their own social, economic and environmental objectives. Closer economic integration of rural areas with neighbouring urban areas can narrow rural-urban disparities, expand opportunities and encourage the retention of skilled people, including youth, in rural areas. There is considerable potential for rural job creation not only in farming, agro-processing and rural industry, but also in building rural infrastructure, sustainable management of natural resources, waste and residues.

The village development aims at the quality of life that is the key factor of sustainable growth in the effectiveness of the agricultural production. To achieve this enhanced production and productivity in the rural areas there must be a spatial balance in the social and economic development. Hence, the main target of the sustainable village development is to bring about improvement in the ecological environment so that it may lead to growth and happiness which thereby encourage the community participation in the process of development. Several poverty alleviation programmes and other developmental programmes have been launched by the Central Government for the rural poor, comprising small and marginal farmers, landless labourers and rural artisans such as Integrated Rural Development Programme (IRDP), National Rural Employment Programme (NREP), Training of Rural Youth for Self Employment ((TRYSEM), Rural Landless Employment Guarantee Programme (RLEGP), Jawahar Gram Samridhi Yojana (JGSY), Antyodaya Programme, etc.

Village Development or Rural Development is the process that seeks social change and sustainable economic development for the rural people and their progress. The ultimate goal is to improve the quality of life of the rural people and preserve the nature and the environment around them.

There are **three basic needs, for the rural development following sustainable future:**

a. **Improving millions of people's welfare that live in the country** (nearly half of the world population), **thus reducing the rural-urban gap,** stamping out poverty and preventing city migration.
b. **Protecting and preserving** natural, landscape and cultural resources.
c. Ensuring **universal access to food** with a sustainable farming production.

The World Monitoring Report of the Millennium Development Goals (2013) confirmed that the **rural-urban gap** still existed in the whole world. Illiteracy, lack of health care or poverty are some of the deep-rooted problems affecting the country. Despite all these, international aid for rural areas has decreased two third in the past decades.

In the present context, the villages in India are dealt with challenges related to access to the basic services, economic opportunities and some degree of incoherence with regard to rural-urban divide. According to the 2011 census, more than 65 per cent of our population lives in rural areas and mostly in the conditions of desperate poverty. The economy of these poor, rural households is directly connected to the village natural resource base—its forests, grazing lands and water resources. Investment in environmental protection, rural infrastructure and rural health and education are important to the sustainable village development and can enhance national well-being. Beyond meeting basic needs, development must be linked to raising productivity and income. The vulnerabilities of the rural poor to the economic and financial crisis and to climate change and water shortage must be addressed. The success of the sustainable village development depends on implementing comprehensive strategies for dealing with climate change, drought, desertification and natural disaster.

Most of the traditional and conventional farm practices are not ecologically sustainable. It leads to the misuse of natural resources, reducing soil fertility, causing soil erosion and contributing to global climate change. But sustainable agriculture has some major advantages over traditional practices. Sustainable agriculture improves fertility and soil structure. It increases the organic matter, content of the topsoil, thus raising its ability to retain and store water that falls as rain. Sustainable agriculture practices involve mixed cropping, thus increasing the diversity of crops produced and raising the diversity of insects and other animals and plants in and around the fields. Sustainable agriculture reduces the use of hazardous chemical and control pests. Conventional agriculture contributes to the production of greenhouse gases in various ways like reducing the amount of carbon stored in the soil and in vegetation, through the production of Methane in irrigated field and production of artificial fertilizers etc. By adopting sustainable agriculture system, one can easily overcome this problem.

Social sustainability in farming techniques is related to the idea of social acceptability and justice. Development cannot be sustainable unless it reduces poverty. Sustainable agriculture practices are useful because it is based on local social customs, traditions and norms etc. Because of being familiar with the local people are more likely to accept and adopt them. Moreover, sustainable agriculture practices are based on traditional know-how and local innovation. Local people have knowledge about their environment, crops and livestock. Traditional agriculture is more gender-oriented, where a woman bears the heaviest burden in terms of labour. Sustainable agriculture ensures that the burden and benefits are shared equitably between man and woman.

Thus, sustainable village development promotes poverty eradication in rural areas, promoting pro-poor planning and budgeting at the national and local levels, and addresses basic needs and enhance provision of and access to services as a precursor to improve livelihoods and as an enabling factor of people's engagement in productive activities and provide social protection programmes to benefit, *inter alia*, the vulnerable households.

One of the successful Sustainable Village Development Model is "Chitrakoot Model of Village Development" led by pioneer Nanaji Deshmukh which is very important for social work professionals to study and apply in their practice settings.

Chitrakoot Model of Sustainable Village Development

Chitrakoot model of sustainable village development was started by Nanaji Deshmukh in the year 2005 in the 80 villages of Uttar Pradesh and Madhya Pradesh. The aim was to achieve self-reliance for these villages. Nanaji integrated programmes for the development of rural areas of Chitrakoot that covers Health, Hygiene, Education, Agriculture, Income generation and Conservation of resources that is both sustainable and replicable. The goal of this project is Total Transformation through total development with people's initiative and participation.

In the same lines, project-WASH by UNICEF works in many countries worldwide to improve water and sanitation services, as well as basic hygiene practices. WASH is the collective term for Water, Sanitation and Hygiene. Due to their interdependent nature, these three core issues are grouped together to represent a growing sector. While each being a separate field of work, it is dependent on the presence of the other. For example, without toilets, water sources become contaminated; without clean water, basic hygiene practices are not possible. Nanaji's ideas of sustainable development from grassroots level is reflected in the modern developmental projects of UNICEF.

Man's physical body is home to his soul. Though perishable, it must be kept healthy and in good condition, in order to achieve its purpose in life. It was an appreciation of this fact that gave birth to the sciences of *Yoga* and *Ayurveda*. *Yoga* links each organ of the body to the organism as a whole—uniting body and soul. *Ayurveda* is the science of longevity, of which curative medicine is only a small part. India's two ancient *Shastras* (sciences), *Yoga* (including Naturopathy) and *Ayurveda*, provide pointers to finding an alternative path, as their main goal has always been the maintenance of lifelong health. These *Shastras* do not treat the body in isolation but treat it as a part of a psycho-physical-intellectual-spiritual continuum.

Deen Dayal Research Institute (DRI) at Chitrakoot has worked on an alternate system of health, i.e.; *Ayurveda*. A centre- 'Arogya Dham' has been established where all the medicines manufactured are in accordance with the Ayurvedic texts. The aim of Arogyadham is to provide lifelong health to all children.

The pregnant women are also given proper advice and counselling about pregnancies, midwifery and children, which includes ideal parenting methods and diets for newborn babies. Arogyadham had also developed a medical kit comprising 35 herbal medicines. All frequently occurring diseases can be treated by these medicines. All these medicines are prepared using locally available herbs and are very cheap. This medical kit has become very popular among the people of these villages. The direction for the use of these medicines is also given along with the kit in very simple language.

In the field of education, DRI has worked on the Model Educational System to make these students self-reliant and integrate them in social activities. It has established *Gurukuls* on the ancient *Gurukul* educational pattern. It has also taken the initiative of evolving an ideal model of pre-primary level quality education. An "Educational Research Centre (ERC)" at Chitrakoot for field-based research to reshape the whole educational system according to the needs of time has been established. The ERC of Chitrakoot educate children of 4-8, 8-12, and 12-16 years of age group through various activities. ERC comprises departments like "Mobile Scientific Laboratories" to demonstrate such experiments that have a direct bearing on rural life, "Computer Software Development" to develop the educational software for rural children.

With the aim of improving livelihood and nutrition security of farmers in the region, Bioversity International in collaboration with Krishi Vigyan Kendras (KVK) at Chitrakoot and Satna, implemented different activities under the 'Seeds for Needs' initiative. Farmers got exposed to more varieties of different crops to understand their quality traits and strengths under different agro-climatic conditions. Though sharing the border, the two districts present very different agro-climatic conditions.

For developing entrepreneurship among rural youth, the focus of Chitrakoot model is the training in product or service development and marketing. Training in entrepreneurship is linked to the dissemination of appropriate technologies for upgrading rural production facilities. Also, a parallel industrialization system capable of providing employment for all by producing quality goods from locally available resources through self-employment and Self Help Groups is also being developed. The focus is to empower women and small-scale farmers and indigenous people, through securing equitable land tenure supported by appropriate legal frameworks. Promote equitable access to land, water, financial resources and technologies by women, indigenous people and other vulnerable groups.

The support is given to provide access to credit and other mechanisms as well as resources for farm-based activities, especially for small-scale farmers, including women in particular. In developing countries to better manage the various risks they face, including price, weather, climate, water shortages, land degradation and natural disasters, including by providing aid and promoting the development of agriculture insurance market.

Nanaji created and developed educational programmes for rural communities aimed at disease prevention, eliminate old and new forms of illiteracy in rural communities and ensure provision of primary education and access to secondary and tertiary educational opportunities as well as vocational and entrepreneurship training including proactive and market-related elements to build capacities within rural communities, in particular for youth, young girls, women and indigenous people. Improved access by rural people and communities to information, education, extension services and learning resources, knowledge and training to support sustainable development planning and decision-making. The energy service was also improved, including renewable and alternative sources of energy for sustainable village development. The access of the rural population to safe drinking water and adequate sanitation was also enhanced.

Nanaji took reliable steps to support the development, transfer and use of safe and environmentally sound construction technologies and practices, in particular for housing, to improve living standards and to create employment in rural areas. Nanaji devoted his entire time to Deendayal Research Institute, established way back in 1969. He had been a member of Rashtriya Swayamsevak Sangh (RSS). He is credited with bolstering Jana Sangh in Uttar Pradesh (UP). He established first Saraswati Shishu Mandir at Gorakhpur in 1950. He has been honoured with Padma Vibhushan in 1999 and with Bharat Ratna in 2019. In the very recent times, Shree Narendra Modi, the prime minister of India paid tribute to Nanaji and praised his organizational skills and efforts to serve society.

References

Kumar, A.S., (2011). *Pandit Deen Dayal Upadhyaya*. Retrieved from https://books.google.co.in/books?id=04JwBgAAQBAJ&pg=PP5&redir_esc=y#v=onepage&q&f=false.

Kakodar, A. (2016). Revisiting S&T inspired Indian model of holistic development.

Nanaji Deshmukh, Sangh ideologue who established RSS in UP (Profile). *Outlook*, India. Retrieved on 29 August 2019.

Scoones, I. (2015). *Sustainable Livelihoods and Rural Development*. Practical Action Publishing.

Shepherd, A. (1998). *Sustainable Rural Development*. London. Palgrave.

Warren, F. (2013). *Practice of Sustainable Community Development: A Participatory Framework for Change*. Springer.

Who was Nanaji Deshmukh? (2017). Retrieved from https://indianexpress.com/article/who-is/who-is-nanaji-deshmukh-4884617//

United Nation Developmental Programme (2020).

7

Social Action

A Replica of Nanaji Deshmukh's Chitrakoot Project of Rural Development

Dimple Mishra

Social action as a process of change to be brought about by deliberate group and community efforts was not unknown to the profession of social work. As early as 1922, Mary Richmond, one of the early pioneers of social work profession, referred to it as one of the four processes in social work. In fact, it is an integral part of the concept of social work arising from the liberalistic, rationalistic and democratic traditions. The early efforts to promote the settlement movement in the USA and to change the system of charities into a programme of family welfare were motivated by a desire to convert the services from ameliorative to curative and promotive.

In 1977, 'Social Action Model' was best incorporated by Nanaji at Chitrakoot with a mission to create a prototype of self-sustaining model of development based on the concept of 'Gram Swaraj'. After initial experiments in Gonda (UP) and Beed (Maharashtra), Nanaji finally fine-tuned an integrated programme for the development of rural areas that covers health, hygiene, education, agriculture, and income generation, conservation of resources and social conscience that is both sustainable and replicable with the aim of achieving self reliance for these villages. Many of the hundreds of villages that have come under what is now popularly known as "Chitrakoot Project", generate their own electricity through the Bio-energy and solar energy plants. The villages which always faced water shortage today have a variety of rain harvesting and water conservation methods. Organic farming is not just for experimentation but a way of life and chemical fertilizers are no more inevitability. Women entrepreneurs today, help run many small scale industries which produce quality goods. All of this with very little support from the Government.

He created change in the system through his dedicated efforts by opting social action as a model in a remote village named Chitrakoot. Due to his continuous efforts he was awarded with *Padma Vibhushan* for his outstanding lifetime work in social service. He was not only a man with good deeds but also an educationist, a social reformer and social activist.

Introduction

In tracing the history of social action one can draw insights from society as well as from developments in the social work profession. Social action is as old as human society. Social Action can be traced from available historical records of the Plebian protest against Rome in the 5th century B.C. from ancient Rome to the Civil Rights movement in the United States it has had a long and varied history. Its examples in the West could be seen in the resistance of the Netherlands to Spanish rule in the mid-sixteenth century, the Boycott by Irish peasants in 1880, Bloody Sunday of 1905 (the Russian Revolution), the East German uprising of 1953, the Hungarian Revolution of 1956 and the Bus Boycott of Afro-Americans in the USA.

In India, Buddhist and later other religious movements emerged as social protest movements. There were always movements against the oppressive rulers in the form of revolts of the masses against the oppressor. Examples in the recent colonial history of India are with reference to the revolts of 1857 against the oppressive economic and political policies that caused famine conditions and unjust land revenue systems, peasant movements of Bardoli and agrarian movements across the nation. These continued beyond post-independence period. Colonial India saw many movements for raising the status of the masses, seeking equality in educational opportunities and fighting against oppressive caste hierarchy and unjust taxation, in various parts of the country.

In compliance to that, Nanaji Deshmukh worked towards the anti-poverty and minimum needs programme. Other areas of his work were agriculture and cottage industry, rural health and rural education. Deshmukh assumed chairmanship of the institute after leaving politics and devoted all his time to building up the institute. He was also instrumental in carrying out social restructuring programme in over 500 villages of both Uttar Pradesh and Madhya Pradesh states of India. He also published the journal "Manthan" (introspection) which was edited by K.R. Malkani for many years. He did social work in Gonda (U.P.), Balrampur and Beed (Maharashtra). The motto of his project was: *"Har hath ko denge kaam, har khet ko denge paanee"*.

He also established Chitrakoot Gramodaya Vishwavidyalaya in Chitrakoot, India's first rural University, and served as its Chancellor. Nanaji implemented the philosophy of integral humanism to improve the living standards of more than 150 villages of Bundelkhand.

Professional Development of Social Action in Social Work

According to Shankar Pathak, in India the developments of the profession began with the establishment of the first school of social work in Bombay in 1936. The model of social work that was imported was the individual-oriented ameliorative professional model. It was felt by many leading writers in the profession that it was highly unsuited to the needs and conditions of Indian society. Because Indian society is group-oriented and collectivistic-oriented—emphasis was on the concept of duties rather than rights. Such concepts emanated from the cultural milieu that was at the same time cosmopolitan (multi-religious, multi-linguistic) as it was sectarian (casteism and communalism). The new emerging profession has to locate itself in this social atmosphere. In Indian philosophical and religious traditions, the concept of social welfare was much wider than the residual content of welfare to the handicapped and weaker sections of society and was much akin to the modern initial view of welfare and included preventive aspects as part of it. In contrast the social welfare model, including the professional model of social work that evolved in USA was influenced by a variety of factors that were specific to its context.

The influence of sociological concepts began to be felt as they appeared in social work literature as a result of development of other major methods of social work—group work and community organization. The individual-oriented approach in social work persisted for quite some time even after this. Pathak identifies the middle of 1980s as a beginning of the reversal of this trend towards increasing professionalization with its associated consequences and a gradual swing back to the earlier social reform orientation. There was an influence of the new concepts on social welfare especially social systems theory. Social reform and social action perspectives began to prevail because of particular social conditions in the US—which may be both internal and external. This had effects on the social welfare institutions in the form of growing sense of democratic factors about the nature of professional techniques and organizational procedures which seemed to take precedence over the needs and interests of clients. Such professional changes taking place in the West had their effects in the developments of the profession in India. Thus, the focus on social reform and social change and social action began to remerge when the Western world began to experience the influence of sociological theories.

Deshmukh's Contribution in the Field of Rural Development

Nanaji Deshmukh was born on October 11th, 1916 in Kadoli, a small town in the Parbhani district of Maharashtra. Though losing his parents at a very early age and confronted severe poverty, he acquired education with many difficulties. He got his higher education at the prestigious Birla Institute of Technology and Science in Pilani. Nanaji was deeply inspired by Lokmanya Tilak and his nationalist ideology. He showed keen interest in social service activities. He established India's first Saraswati Shishu Mandir at Gorakhpur in 1950. It reflects Nanaji's love for education and knowledge.

Inspired by Lokmanya Tilak, Nanaji acquired interest in social service and activities. Deshmukh actively participated in Bhoodan movement started by Vinoba Bhave. When Jaiprakash Narayan gave the call for "Total Revolution", he responded by giving total support to this movement. When the Janata Party was formed, Nanaji was one of its main architects. Janata Party stormed into power by sweeping off the Congress and Nanaji was elected from Balrampur parliamentary constituency in Uttar Pradesh. When he was offered ministerial berth by the then Prime Minister, Shri Morarjee Desai, he politely refused it. For him politics was never a career but a mission. He was not the person who would stick to politics or officialdom whatever may be. Of his own volition he announced his retirement from politics in presence of Jaiparaksh Narayan and since then never looked back. By spending 2 months with Vinoba, he was inspired by the success and appeal of the movement.

After retirement from active politics in 1972, Deshmukh then founded Deendayal Research Institute to validate the philosophy of integral humanism propounded by Pandit Deendayal Upadhyaya. Deshmukh developed a model for the development of rural areas on the basis of integral humanism. Integral Humanism gave a vision for Bharat that, with an approach to man and his relationship to society that is integral and complementary, could transform Bharat into a self-reliant and compassionate example for the world to follow. Nanaji implemented the philosophy of integral humanism to improve the living standard of more than 150 villages of Bundelkhand.

Deendayal Research Institute's Chitrakoot Project is an integrated and holistic model for the development of rural India, based on the principles outlined in Pt. Deendayal Upadhyaya's Integral Humanism to create a society based on the complementarity of the family, primary school and the local population. The Chitrakoot Project is a self-reliance campaign that was launched on 26th January, 2002 and covers 500 villages around Chitrakoot in 2 phases. The campaign has also been started in the villages covered by the Institute in Gonda and Beed districts.

The self-reliance campaign covers all aspects of individual, family and societal life of the villagers. The key to the campaign is the concept of Samaj Shilpi Dampati (SSD), 'graduate' couples that lives within the villages itself, and are responsible for motivating and guiding a cluster of 5 villages.

Foremost among the aspects covered is income generation. This is achieved by introducing watershed and soil management techniques where necessary; new and improved farming technologies through 2.5 and 1.5 acre model farms that enable small and marginal farmers—who account for 80 per cent of the rural population—to look after the family needs and save; and by increasing Non-Farm Sector incomes through entrepreneur training and the formation of income-generating Self Help Groups (SHGs) that are both stand alone, and vertically integrated.

Issues of health and hygiene are the second most important aspect of the campaign, as an unhealthy individual is incapable of working to improve his/her economic condition. Regardless of the manifold benefits of Ayurveda and Naturopathy—Allopathic intervention—when the ratio of doctors to population is in excess of 1:10,000 and the cost of medicine high is impractical. Therefore, in issues related to health, the Chitrakoot Project looks to *Ayurveda* and Naturopathy to keep villagers healthy. Locally available herbs and nutritional vegetable gardens are the key interventions used in this area, including a *Dadima ka Butua*, a collection of 34 *Ayurvedic* local herbs and preparations that can be used to treat common ailments. Where *Ayurveda* is not applicable, as for example in Dentistry, state-of-the-art facilities have been provided at Arogyadham, Deendayal Research Institute's Ayurvedic & Naturopathy Hospital & Research Centre at Chitrakoot.

Illiteracy and social consciousness is the third area covered by the campaign. A 'functional literacy campaign' developed by TCS is being conducted for the villagers by the *Samaj Shilpi Dampati*, our Educational Research Centre and the 4 schools that operate within the Project area. Ram Darshan, a unique museum that highlights socially relevant aspects of Lord Rama's life helps villagers inculcate human values to encourage them to live in a spirit of co-operation and harmony with each other.

Later, Nanaji established Chitrakoot Gramodaya Vishvavidyalaya, India's first rural University, in Chitrakoot. For suitably running these projects, he developed couples inclined towards social service into *Samaj Shilpis* (sculptors of society). These *Samaj Shilpis* are devotedly handling the projects and executing them correctly and in good speed.

Nanaji was also the first chancellor of Chitrakoot University. The Government of India bestowed on him the Padma Vibhushan for his outstanding lifetime work in social service. After living a long and inspiring life of a social entrepreneur, Nanaji Deshmukh breathed his last on 27th February, 2010 at the premises of Chitrakoot Gramodaya Vishwavidyalaya. He is remembered by the country as a great leader, a social activist, an educationist and also as an inspiring social entrepreneur.

Chitrakoot Project of Rural Development

Social Reconstruction

Chitrakoot symbolizes the challenging summation of the experiments conducted and the experiences gained through the earlier ventures in Gonda and Beed. Chitrakoot is a small township bordering UP and MP, 120 miles south of Allahabad. The villages around are predominantly tribal and backward in spite of the availability of rich resources like forest wealth and agricultural products. Lord Ram started upliftment of the downtrodden from this historic place.

Nanaji to his credit has several firsts. The conception of Gramodaya Vishwavidhyalaya (Rural University) is one of them. It was established with the objectives of overall development of the students to make them self-reliant and confident so that they can generate their livelihood through their acquired skills and more importantly to involve every member of the University-teaching, non-teaching and the students in the rural development programmes.

Chitrakoot Gramodaya Vishwavidyalaya was established on 12th February, 1991 and Shri Nanaji provided his leadership and guidance for three and half years as chancellor. This is the first rural University in India with twenty faculties providing facilities for higher education. After some time some section of society grew jealous and the funding was stopped by the then government for unnecessary reasons. Nanaji graciously relinquished the office of chancellor and transferred all assets of the University to the state government in the larger interest of students and teaching and non-teaching staff.

List of Chitrakoot Projects

Aarogyadham

Clinical

Nidan Sadan (Out Patients Department).
Swasthya Sadan (In Patients Department).
Dental Department.
Rural Health Department.
Matri Sadan (Maternity Ward).
Yoga Sadan (Yoga & Naturopathy Department).

Non-Clinical

Ayurveda Sadan (Research Laboratories).
Herbal Garden.
Landscaping.
Library
Ahar Vihar Sadan (Dietetic unit).

Udyamith Vidyapeeth (TPC): TPC is a well known unit in Gonda and Balrampur districts, which played a vital role in promotion of bee keeping through training and supply of boxes. Total 130 persons have been trained, they started working with the help of Bank loan and formation of Self-Help Group (SHG). More than 50 trained youth have been earning Rs. 30,000–Rs. 40,000 per year in rural areas.

Watershed Management: The watershed management has given the villages, an economic benefit that is far greater than the sum of its parts. This has changed overall scenario of the treated area with increase in water level, increased agricultural and forest produce production; increased employment opportunities.

A significant change in land use has taken place. Watershed development in the village resulted in significant increase in area under cultivation (132.91%). The culturable wastelands and fallow lands have decreased by 26.67 per cent and 96.62 per cent respectively.

An increase of 480.31 per cent in irrigated area was observed. An increase of 2.83 m and 3.0 m in ground water table was observed in the month of May and December.

Increased irrigation facilities and improved crop demonstrations encouraged the farmers to adopt new crop production technologies, which significantly increased the yield of crops by 27.01 to 131.7 per cent.

The productivity of paddy, wheat, gram and mustard has increased by 53.24 per cent, 43.25 per cent, 58.02 per cent and 68.40 per cent respectively. The area under improved varieties increased from 12.2 ha to 1980. 5 ha. A perceptible improvement was observed in the quality of life.

The average family income became doubled within a short period of 3 years. Improvement in the economic conditions, led change in attitude of tribal families towards the education, health, environmental protection, human right, self-realization for future production and cooperative life.

In the beginning of the project where only 55 children were noticed to go school, but with improvement of lifestyle of villagers in the area in 2007, 1174 students were recorded to seek education. Even most of the tribal families have started to send their children in Chitrakoot and Satna for better education.

Villagers have realized awareness about environmental protection as a result more forest restoration is visible. The GDP of these 18 villages was observed to increase by 82.41 per cent and the watershed development programme was found to be economically viable.

Resource Centre: Resource Centre was established with the following missions:

1. To implement and maintain Quality Management System in the organization.

2. To continuously improve the processes of all the projects and QMS, and to implement systems to monitor the effectiveness of all the processes.
3. To automate MIS and SIS so that management can get immediate information regarding the status of the villages at any point of time.
4. To develop a data warehouses and data mining system to manage the huge data of 500 villages.
5. To set up "IT enabled" knowledge management system/ Village Knowledge centre.
6. To capture the intellectual properties of DRI generated by Hon. Nanaji, social scientists, agriculture scientists etc. and make it available at a touch of a button for transfer for the benefit of mankind for many more years to come.
7. To develop a visible, transparent, self-explanatory system of achievement for all the projects of DRI.
8. To develop 'Sustainable Village Development' training modules for other voluntary organizations, business houses, government and developing and underdeveloped countries.

Ram Darshan: Its purposes are following:

- Ramdarshan also plays an important part in the Self-Reliance Campaign for making villages dispute free. This year, disputes were amicably resolved at 20 self-reliance centres through the intervention of volunteers of Ram Darshan and local social architect couple (Samaj Shilpi Dampati).
- During Deepawali, Ram Darshan remained open for 16 hours a day for 5 days and had 19,354 visitors, including 741 children. In an innovative experiment, a 45 minute V.C.D. was produced for visitors and three different sized photographs are also made available for the devotees.

Krishi Vigyan Kendra Ganiva, Chitrakoot: Following strategies were opted:

- Emphasizes dry land farming based on current situation of Bundelkhand agroclimatic condition.
- To motivate farmers for water and moisture conservation to fight against drought and water scarcity.
- Increase the area and productivity of pulse crop up to 10-15 per cent and 30-40 per cent respectively under rain-fed cropping system.
- To promote organic farming for improvement in soil health and productivity for sustainable agriculture.
- Popularization of diversified agricultural model among farming community.
- Breed improvement of low productive animals to increase productivity.
- Promotion of off-season vegetable cultivation.
- Production of good quality fish seed to enhance fish production.
- Women empowerment through backyard poultry and kitchen gardening.

Surendrapaul Gramodaya Vidyalaya: Strategies are as follows:

- To establish the economic viability of indigenous cattle of society.
- To conserve the indigenous breed by in-suite method.
- To maintain the cow population at farmer's door with enhanced potentiality by providing pure high potential tested (on the basis of reproductive, productive and physical traits) bulls for breeding.
- To develop replicable model of the sustainable Gaushala.

Gurukul Sankul: Yaganukul Educational Reconstruction. The age to which our pre-primary level school going children belong (i.e., from three to five years), is best suited for promoting their observational qualities that add to their capability of mental receptivity through the approach of learning while playing. At this age, the role of teachers should be to act as facilitators of the learning process. It is worth considering that the children going to

Nanhi Duniya (another project) leave their family environment for the first time.

Chitrakoot Ras Shala: To bring total transformation and development of the society through designing and implementing a framework to achieve sustained self-reliance in villages through the initiative involvement and empowerment of the villagers with replicable, definable and tangible parameters.

Govansh Vikas Evam Anusandhan: Vermi-composting is an eco-friendly, socially sound and economically viable innovative technology to manage the organic waste resources on low capital input basis. This does not call for expensive laboratories or sophisticated industrial instruments. It has multiple benefits—can convert wastes in rich manure for soil or plant and can eliminate the dependence on chemicals. It is basically a process of composting with earth worms (*Eisenia foetida*). It can be done virtually anywhere either in-door or out-door conditions. Organic wastes used for composting are cow dung, agricultural waste, forestry waste, city leaf, litter etc.

Krishi Farm: Purpose is to provide improved seed to the farmers and motivate them to enhance the production of crops by adopting improved package of practices.

Krishi Vignan Kendra Majhgawan, Satna (MP).

Ramnath Ashram Shala: Established with the following objectives:

Since ancient time Chitrakoot has been an area being primarily dominated by forest dwellers, the tribal people who are the native inhabitants. This section of the society suffers miserably from poverty, ignorance and ill health. Since its inception on 15th August, 1992, Ramnath Ashramshala, Chitrakoot, actively engaged in the all-round personality development of the young generation of these people. It provides completely free of cost residential education, boarding and lodging facility to 100 tribal girls and 100 tribal boys. It is committed to the cause of inculcating the sense of social sensitivity in the sons and daughters of the tribal people so that they become responsible citizen of society in future.

a. Organizing science teachers programme in the 50 km. radial area around the Chitrakoot with the help of other institutions/organization.
b. Demonstration of the life-related science experiment and educational CDs through mobile science lab.

Children are the life-stream of a nation. It is only through the proper development of the young, that the foundation of a strong nation and dynamic society can be laid on solid ground. Bearing this premise in mind, a new educational pattern should have been evolved in free India. Unfortunately, the government, from the very beginning, ignored initiatives for children. This has resulted in a situation that has had a disastrous impact on the natural process for the blossoming of our budding citizens.

Krishna Devi Vanavasi Balika Vidyalaya: Project mission are:

1. All-round development of the downtrodden Scheduled Tribe students through education, training and good conduct.
2. Extension and dissemination of education in tribal villages so as to join them with the national stream.
3. To develop this institute as a role model for the other educational institutes.

Paramanand Ashram Paddhati Vidyalaya: Its objectives are as follows:

For the benefit of the boys and girls of Scheduled Caste, a school was started on 9th July, 2000 at Ganivan village under the name Parmanand Ashram Paddhati Vidyalaya. The school provides co-education with separate residential accommodation to boys and girls. There are about 100 students in all in the school. The students are taught not only the syllabus prescribed by the Govt. of Uttar Pradesh (U.P.) but also various extra-curricular activities are undertaken to help them in physical and mental development. The students are prepared in all respects to compete with the students of other communities.

1. To provide life beneficial character and moral building education from primary to higher secondary level.
2. To create the favourable atmosphere of education for the holistic development of the ST & SC boys and Girl students.

Jan Shikshan Sansthan has the following objectives:

1. Skill development and life enrichment education of those who are in the age group of 15-35 years having no or rudimentary levels of education.

2. The skill development centre is aimed at improving the skill and quality of life of its beneficiaries. Though the scheme does not target any specific group or area it concentrates on the socially-economically backward and educationally disadvantaged group of urban/rural population such as neo-literates, semi-literates, SC, ST, women and girls, slum dwellers, migrant workers etc.

3. Deendayal Research Institute has three Jan Shikshan Sansthan at Ganivan, Chitrakoot (U.P.), Gandhi Park, Gonda (U.P.) and Beed (Maharashtra).

4. The objective of JSS is not only the economic well-being of participants but also it fosters the qualitative aspect of human life pertaining to behaviour and attitude.

Therefore, it conducted activities to create an environment where people started seeking the correct information and option for betterment of their lives.

Conclusion

Social work in a developing country ought to go beyond the role of dispenser of social welfare services or a therapeutic agent. Social action is any action taken by an organized group or movement to achieve some reform or to promote a particular cause, outside the normal or formal channels of a government or political system, and aimed at gaining support from the wider public. The rise of public interest litigation and citizen action groups has given space and highlighted the need for and widened the scope for social action. Social work as a profession has its core values as social justice and equality. Social action is the method advocated to achieve this. Thus, it can be used in conjunction with the other methods of social work practice for effective goal achievement.

According to Nanaji Deshmukh's Chitrakoot model of rural development, social action has been seen through varied perspectives. Earlier social action was seen as a protective method of social work, whereas through Deshmukh's contribution towards chitrakoot model of rural development, we can see it in its originality i.e., perfect model for social work. Whether he worked against poverty, health, education, medication etc., his contributions in any sector related for the welfare of the society is the best replicable model of social action for social work.

References

Siddiqui, H.Y. (1984). *Social Work and Social Action,* New Delhi, Harnam Publications.

Dunham, A. (1970). *The New Community Organisation,* New York, Thomas. Y. Cromwell.

Pathak, S. (1981). *Social Welfare,* Delhi, Macmillan.

MSW-001, IGNOU. *Origin and Development of Social Work.*

8

Nanaji Deshmukh

A Great Architect of Conflict-free Society

Geeta Sahare

Nanaji Deshmukh was a multifaceted social revolutionary. He is an exemplary that how a son of poor parents and born in a small village could become a noted leader and inspiration to thousands of his followers. His life and work is an example of how technology and traditional values could be synchronised towards common goals of human welfare and mass empowerment. His ideas of self-sufficient villages, he not only perceived but also brought into practice by establishing Deendayal Research Institute at Chitrakoot in Uttar Pradesh and made several villages self-reliant. It is very difficult to write about such great personality Bharat Ratna Nanaji Deshmukh in few words, therefore, I could make only a few comments only. It is a tribute to a great visionary.

Early Life and Achievements

The Jan Sangh veteran, Chandikadas Amritrao Deshmukh is popularly better known as Nanaji Deshmukh. He was so popular by this title name Nanaji that many people might not even know his real name. Not many people would even have thought that a child born in the era of British-India on 11 October, 1916 would be a great social reformer that he earned Padma Vibhushan in 1999 and later was awarded Bharat Ratna, India's highest civilian award in 2019 posthumously. Even his Class V teacher in the primary school at home village Kadoli, in Parbhani district near Aurangabad in Maharashtra won't have thought about it when he whipped him for shouting "*Vande Mataram*" while the freedom struggle was still going on.

He joined the RSS Shakha at the age of thirteen, moved by the way RSS protected Hindus in the 1926 Nagpur riots and grew up to believe that RSS was the medium to the nation's independence and all type of salvation of human kind. Nanaji was amongst the first people from the RSS sent to work for the Jana Sangh in the period after the country's independence. Once he himself explained, "I am saddened by the manner in which the term Hindutva is being misused. Every political party needs something to propagate, to win votes."

Inspiration to Young Generation

Nanaji brought smiles in the hundreds of thousands people in the nation. Nanaji had a precise understanding of opportunities and challenges of the Indian villages and his deep compassion made him realise the problems of a common man. His work will always live in our memories for his transformation approach to integrated and value-based empowerment of the human being and this article is a reflection of the work and achievement of the great soul.

Nanaji's love for education and knowledge was reflected in his creation of India's first Shishu Mandir in 1950. Nanaji actively participated in agricultural land reform movement started by Vinoba Bhave, a contemporary of Mahatma Gandhi. By spending two months with Vinoba he was inspired by the success and appeal of the movement. Nanaji devoted his entire time to Deendayal Research Institute that he established way back in 1969 and organized rural development in Chitrakoot region.[1] He established Chitrakoot Gramodaya Vishwavidyalaya in Chitrakoot, India's first rural university and was its first Vice-Chancellor.

Ideas about Self-reliant Villages

Nanaji Deshmukh and his team worked towards the empowerment of the rural regions of central India covering over 500 villages and implementing a village development model, which is most suited for Indian conditions. They enabled about a 100 villages to be self-reliant. They devised a unique way to define self-reliance in the villages which not only take into account economic development and poverty alleviation but also socio-cultural aspects. This includes the village being litigation free, harmonious and improvement in the condition of women and value addition to the lifestyles of all constituents of the society. So, we can say that Nanaji was the most perfectionist when it came to its approach of societal development. He had a strong belief in the capacity of the youth to be the sculptures of the future and builders of the nation, his life and work is an example of how technology and traditional values could be synchronised towards common goals of human welfare and mass empowerment. Nanaji Deshmukh was someone who rose above party politics and his mission of social service cut across all party lines and gathered people and political leaders from all dimensions towards the great mission of development. His life is that of nurturing nobility of the leadership and perseverance through constant innovation of achieving socio-economic development.[2]

Architect of Anti-emergency Struggle

Nanaji Deshmukh who was General Secretary of the Lok Sangharsh Samiti and the main force behind Jayaprakash Narayan's agitation for Total Revolution. During emergency, they were publishing underground news bulletins and pamphlets in all the languages of the country in order to break the censor barrier; setting up underground cells at several levels to contact workers and the public; staging protest demonstrations and later organizing a *satyagraha* movement from November 14, 1975 to January 26, 1976 in state capitals and districts; raising funds to feed the movement; rendering all possible help to the families of detenes and prospective *satyagrahis* and keeping in touch with those in jail; organizing a protest movement among the Indian communities abroad and feeding the foreign press with the true state of affairs in the country and last but not the least, to keep the movement scrupulously non-violent.

Nanaji's Ideas of Hindutva

At the age of 80, in self-imposed exile from public life since 1978, he was running rural development projects in Uttar Pradesh at Gonda and Chitrakoot—a place bordering Madhya Pradesh chosen because he believed Lord Ram started his odyssey to restore the rule of law from here—and Beed in Maharashtra. But for Nanaji, disillusioned yet determined, his life's mission—even as many former pro-Hindutva compatriots strive to rule at the Centre—is the search for his version of Utopia: the "real" India.

"I want to show that better work can be done without being in power," said Nanaji, the son of poor parents, who bases his social work with the poor mostly in the tribal districts, by providing basic health and education, for example: a residential school for over 200 tribal children in Chitrakoot. It is a hard-won conviction. His single-minded devotion to Hindutva as he saw it won him grudging respect within the RSS.

One of the most vocal RSS members and later as the Jana Sangh activist when it was formed in 1951, he always talked animatedly about the message that he tried to spread in the Sangh heyday of the 1960s and 1970s: freedom for the oppressed masses and self-respect. He also believed that Muslims are no different than Hindus. It is because of him only the Jana Sangh prided itself on having numerous Muslim members. "Hindutva is a way of life", he used to say when asked about the similarity of the past and the present fundamentalist colours of the Sangh-evolved BJP and its ultra-right wing constituents, including his political alma mater.[3]

"I am saddened by the manner in which the term Hindutva is being misused these days. Every political party needs something to propagate, to win votes." He added: "Nowadays, nobody leaves politics unless they are literally shoved out." Nobody who knew Nanaji would be surprised. He had always spoken his mind and done things his way, ranging from allegedly promoting RSS cadre in institutions funded by public money to indulging in a politics so Machiavellian that Indira Gandhi often referred to him as the Chanakya of modern Indian politics and Ram Bahadur Rai also described him as "he was the Vinoba of Jana Sangh ideology". At the forefront of every major Sangh demonstration, he was the party's General Secretary along with Atal Bihari Vajpayee in 1976-77.[4]

The Rare Politician and Ideal Personality

He was a very active politician and has played important role in Indian politics. He was instrumental in forging the Janata Party coalition. But when was offered the industry portfolio by the post-Emergency Janata Party government of Morarji, he declined. Nanaji was a "rare politician" who had voluntarily abdicated politics after reaching the age of 60 since it was a time when he could have ripped many fruits, his courage of conviction was so strong that he left active politics when he was almost at the pinnacle.[5] He was the unique personality and all the politicians of the present era can learn and take inspiration from Nanaji Deshmukh. Nitin Gadkari said, "Nanaji was one of the early architects of Jana Sangh and firmly stood for value-based politics. He could rightly be described idealism personified." He was also against the religion-based politics. "They ran the government like their fiefdom", recalled Nanaji. In 1978, he moved to Chitrakoot, activating projects through the Deen Dayal Research Institute, an NGO he set up in 1972 in Delhi. During this time, he still put pursuing 16-20 hours a day, a man in the autumn of his life but with a spring in his step, meeting and advising a steady stream of people—a volunteer who needs guidance about a project, a *Sadhu* who needs legal help—and catching up with correspondence, planning a dairy farm and an *Ayurveda* and naturopathy institute in Chitrakoot. Nanaji thus was a real *Karmyogi*.

Tribute to Nanaji: A Great Rashtrarishi

"My main goal was positive development of society through politics. That didn't work. But positive development of society is a must", he said. It's a belief. It's as simple as that. He was committed to the overall development of villages and his constructive work was the inspiration to the all different Non-governmental organisations. He believed had Pandit Nehru listened to the ideas of Mahatma Gandhi about development and self-sufficiency of village, India's political and economic picture could have been very different. Such a magnificent and multifaceted personality left us for his heavenly abode on 27 February, 2010 but Nanaji's memories would always inspire us as an example of a son of poor parents could become Bharat Ratna by his untiring selfless work and contributed immensely in nation building. "His life's works will forever inspire the new generation in the whole country towards patriotism, sacrifice and service", says Mohan Bhagwat.[6] L.K. Advani said, "we all remembered him for his remarkable role in nation building and his decades-long unblemished public life an indelible impression on his head and heart."[7] Atal Bihari Vajpayee said, "He was an expert in handling challenges. There was a magnetic attraction in his personality and whoever came in touch with him remained with him throughout."[8]

He worked on several projects such as solar lighting of several villages, rural health and education-related services, fund raising efforts help by Rotary International, Tata Energy Research Institute and the multiplying effect. Nanaji used to invite many important people, not only from Delhi but also from other parts of the country. Many of them used to stay at the guest house like George Fernandes, Chandrasekhar, Madhu Dandavate, B.D. Jatti, Karan Singh and many others of high eminence were frequent visitors. He used to hold personal talk on matters of great importance. He was a very hard taskmaster who spared neither himself nor those who worked with him. Nanaji's room had no chairs or tables. It was simple, but elegant and truly reflected his personal style. He used to squat on the carpet. For writing he had a small desk, though his headquarters was Deendayal Research Institute, New Delhi, his heart was away in rural areas he had selected for development work in Gonda District, UP, was his prime location. He had also selected rural areas in Maharashtra and Bihar. He had to keep in close touch with those distant areas and most of his time he spent there, travelling, planning, executing and overseeing the various development projects—most of them quite original and innovative. The idea of deploying young married couples as life workers (*jeevanvritis)* was the brain-child of the hard-core pragmatist in Nanaji. He knew from his experience in RSS that it was difficult to get life workers when would remain bachelors all through. Even more, for working in a rural society, among the common people married couples be more natural and suitable. The only concern was they should have deep dedication to live a life with utter devotion.

He had wide contacts with the great industrialists who had also immense respect for him. They trusted his sincerity and commitment to poor. Nanaji very well knew the fine art of raising money from such sources and spending it in the poverty-stricken rural areas for welfare of the villagers. He travelled a lot and he also knew how to delegate authority to trusted persons of different levels. It was Nanaji's fame and effect that anyone who is invited would be feel it as honour to come and participate. Towering personalities like Morarji Desai, Swami Ranganathananda, Justice Chandrachood, Justice V.R. Krishna Iyer, many vice chancellors and eminent academics had visited in his prestigious programs[9].

Narendra Modi, Hon'ble prime minister of India also remembered that he had the good fortune to work with Nanaji, whom he described as one having a vision and the will to translate vision into action.[10] RSS Chief Mohan Bhagwat also said that Nanaji's life's works will forever inspire the new generations in the whole country towards patriotism, sacrifice and service.[11] In true sense, Nanaji was great a social activist, but he was not one in the usually accepted sense of the term. Social activists of today's paradigm, Nanaji was really different. He was a system builder on a truly *Bharatiya* system based on our cultural and spiritual values, tuned to the needs and requirements of the present situation. That is what he attempted in Gonda, worked in the establishment of mini Rama Rajya that is his real contribution. He was very close to Gandhiji and Guruji than any so-called social activists.

Notes

1. *Rashtra Rishi Nanaji* (2011). OAPM, Oxis and Print Media India Limited, Mumbai.
2. A.P.J. Abdul Kalam said in his speech in Chennai, September 2006.

3. "Architect of anti-emergency struggle", *The Indian Express*, 28th February 2010, New Delhi.
4. Arun Jaitley, Former Rajya Sabha Member in "Kindling a Movement", March 2010, *The Indian Express*.
5. "Nanaji Ki Viraasat", Ratan N. Tata, *Dainik Jaagaran*, 14th March, 2010.
6. Mohan Bhagwat, *Lokmat Times*, 1st March 2010.
7. L.K. Advani in his speech, *The Pioneers*, 1st March 2010, p. 16
8. Atal Bihari Vajpayee, *The Hindu*, February 28th, 2010.
9. Parmeshwaram, P. (2010). "Nanaji: Some Reminiscences", *Organiser*, March 14, p. 9/42.
10. Correspondent, *Lokmat Times*, March, 01, 2010, "Nanaji ended sangh untouchability".
11. *Outlook*, February, 28, 2010.

9
Sewa, Social Service and Social Development—Nanaji Way

Divyanshu Kumar and *Kumar Satyam*

Introduction

The word "*Sewa*" is a Sanskrit word often associated with the aspect of yoga meaning "Service". However, it is more than just a simple desire to help others. As Swami Niranjan explains it, "*Sewa*" is actually composed of two words, "Saha", which means "with that" and "ewa," which means "too". Adding to this, the word "*Sewa*" means "together with" and describes the actions that seek well-being of masses with proper understanding of the needs of others. This should base on togetherness and integration of the society. Though the selfless action we attain the height of realization and higher level of consciousness. At the same time, the practice of *Sewa* becomes a way of self-realization (Yogamour, 2019).

Notion of *Sewa*

Sewa may be a universal construct, which involves performing an act of kindness without expectation of rewards. It is performed selflessly and without any secret motive. As a plan, *Sewa* is embedded in Indian traditions, and is actively promoted by totally different cultures and faiths—because the core belief is that the same—to sacrifice some time and resources for the benefits of others without expectation of anything in return (Sewauk, 2019). According to M.C. Satyanarayan, *Sewa* or service to the poor and suffering is a principle advocated by all religious faiths. To serve the poor and afflicted is enjoyed as a duty of human beings whatever be his religious faith.

Sewa has been described as *dharma* in Hindu culture: '*Sewa* Hi Paramo Dharmah' (सेवा ही परमो धर्म), it means *sewa* is the supreme duty. *Dharma* has three meanings. The first meaning is duty, the second is nature and the third one is concept on which a society sustains. *Sewa* is *dharma* by all these meanings (Bhagwat, 2019). In Hindu tradition, *sewa* is nature of life. Because a human being has soul (atma) and soul is omnipotent. That same is the supreme soul (paramatma) in everyone. Because of this, there is a feeling of affinity in human beings. This affinity manifests naturally. That is why *Sewa* is a nature. In Hinduism, in particular, our ancient seers have gone in great depth into this principle and have laid down guidelines which are distinctive features of Hindu thoughts and philosophy. Our *rishis* (saint) have thought about *sewa* as well as with queries like what is *sewa*, why *sewa*, how *sewa* is done, to whom is *sewa* to be done, what is the best kind of *sewa*, to what extent should a human being do *sewa* and so on. Some of these questions have been answered by them in a unique way. Sewa is a distinct trait of the Hindu culture. We all are an integral part of the society and we imbibe the sense of belongingness to the society since childhood (Abhyankar, 2019).

Sewa: Service to Humanity

Sewa is Sanskrit word that describes the act of selfless service. *Sewa* is an act of compassion and care for others above oneself. The sacred Hindu text, the *Bhagavad Gita*, encourages selfless service, as a way to develop spirituality; thus it is closely linked to the concept of *Karma Yoga*. Unlike other forms of *yoga* which may focus on performing *asana* to transform the physical body, performing *Sewa* is said to transform the personality (Yogapedia, 2019). As we know that in our Hindu concept *Hindutva* means "service to humanity" that all the Hindus are devoted to provide service to the humanity which is known as *Sewa*. *Sewa* is taken into account a distinct form of human *Dharma* in Hindu thought. *Sewa dharma* is a duty. But if one thinks deeply, the concept of *Sewa* is deep and difficult to comprehend in its entirety. Service that is given inconsiderately of something reciprocally, at the right place and time to one that is qualified with the feeling that it is one that is qualified, with the sensation that it's one's duty is considered the character of goodness (*Bhagavad Gita*, 17.20).

सेवा-धर्मः परम गहनो योगिना मप्यगम्यं
SEWA DHARMA PARAMA GAHANO YOGINA MAPYAGAMYAM

It is said that *Sewa* is a very deep concept which even sages find it difficult to understand. But for a common man they have put it in simple words by saying "*paropkarayapunyay, papaya parapeedanam*" परोपकारयपुण्य, पापयापरापीड़नं, i.e. whatever conduces to the great of others is noble deed and will be followed. By the term *Sewa*, the common understanding is that it implies an act, word or thought which helps to mitigate the sufferings of others and increases their happiness.

Sewa: Feeling of Humanitarian Drive

"The same god who is present in me is also present in other human beings. Therefore, serving another individual or a being is serving God. Doing *sewa* is to worship God and to figure for one's salvation and supreme eternal happiness." The motives that inspire human beings to do an act of *sewa* have been varied and many. The feeling of compassion, feeling of humanity, and sympathy are usually mentioned as reasons why human beings do *sewa*. All these motives imply that the server and therefore the served square measures are separate and distinct entities.

ईश्वरः सर्वभूतानां हृद्देशेऽर्जुन तिष्ठति।
ISWARAH SARVABHUTANAM HRADDESHEARJUNA TISHTHATI

The same god who is present in me is also present in other human being or a being is serving god. Doing *Sewa* is to worship God and to work for one's salvation and ultimate eternal happiness. So *Sewa* is furnished for one's own happiness and progress. This was expressed beautifully by Swami Vivekananda who preached the worship of the poor. It is said that serving man is serving God; **Nara Sewa, Narayana Sewa** (नरसेवा, नारायणसेवा)

Hence, those serving the needy, illiterate and deprived should remember that they are serving God in various forms. One must do this work selflessly, without harbouring the feeling of doing a favour and without any ego. One should treat every person as a good soul. One should assume that greatness in that person is dormant and we have got the opportunity to serve him/her. This approach will help us to work without ego (Joshi, 2019). The *Rishis*, Sages and Saints of our Ancient Country Bharata have always considered the entire humanity as one family, without making any discrimination of various nationalities, colour, race, region, language and ways of life of people inhibiting this mother earth and have earnestly declared "Vasudhaiva kutumbakam" (वसुधैव कुटम्बकं)—the whole world is one family. The dictum of "unity in diversity" is one among the distinctive and greatest gifts of the Hindu thought to human society (Parivartan, 2010).

Today, the needs are many, but so is our strength. Let our commitment remain strong. "*Society is our God and service is our worship*" be the underlying principle and "act rather than preach" should take us forward on our path of social transformation (Joshi, 2019).

> It's our firm belief and moral principle that those dirty, illiterate and foolish looking people are our Gods (Narayana). Their worship itself is our social and human religion. That 'man', who is literally sheltered less and devoid of any possession and is the centre of our faith and worship; is the standard major of our contemplation efforts and success. —***Pandit Deendayal Upadhyaya***

Sewa: Performance of Humanitarian Drive

Our seers have said that *Sewa* is done in three ways—*Tana* (Physical aspects of *sewa*), *Mana* (mental aspects of *sewa*), *Dhana* (material aspect of *sewa*); *Sewa* namely through one's mind and through one's wealth. No *Sewa* is complete if it is not done in these three ways. Service through one's body implies physical service, and making all efforts to help suffering person/beings. Service through the mind consists in wondering the mitigation of sorrow and misery, talking about it to others in order to motivate them to do *Sewa*, expression of the *Sewa* feeling through art, literature, drama and other means (BBC, 2019).

Service through wealth is sharing one's own resources—money and material with others. But we have a tendency to see samples of this comprehensive *sewa* in actual life conjointly. If one observes how a mother serves her child, it becomes evident that she devotes a lot of time and physical efforts for the comfort and well-being of the child. Whatever she may be doing or whatever she may be, her child is always in her thought. Whenever the kid speaks, plays or eats she takes a great pleasure in it and sometimes feels that her child is Lord Krishna himself in her home. Serving her kid is serving Lord Krishna, God himself.

Sewa: Application of Humanitarian Drive

"The scope for *sewa* in Hindu thought is incredibly wide. It extends to all or any beings whether or not human, animal, birds, plants or any other". It extends to the surroundings and points out the thrill in living harmonious with nature and within the angle of "live and let live", our scriptures contain many examples of this service—service to mother, father, guests, friends, animals, birds, and other human beings. *Sewa Dharma* continues since the ancient time i.e.:

> न त्वहं कामये राज्यं न स्वर्गं नापुनर्भवम् ।
> कामये दुःखतप्तानां प्राणिनामार्तिनाशनम् ।।
> NA TVAHAM KAMAYE RAJYAM NA SWARGAM
> NAPUNARBHAVAM. KAAMAYE DUKHA-TAPTANAM
> PRANINAMARTI NAASHANAM.

Means, I do not want any kingdom, or heaven or even escape from rebirth. I do desire that the afflictions of all beings tormented by pain in life may cease. All know this story from Bhagavatam. Therefore, our ideal of service is quite old. Our family and our society operate on this feeling of *Sewa*. Since we forgot this tradition there has been deterioration both in the family and the society during the last 2000 years. The absence of *Sewa dharma* means human beings getting selfish and having discriminatory nature.

Utmost *Sewa*: Highest Degree of Satisfaction

The best quiet *Sewa* is one that's eluded the expectation of any reward, return, name or fame, one that does not destroy the self-respect and confidence of sentiments of the beneficiary, the one that helps a beneficiary to help himself. It is said in *Bhagvad Gita* (chapter 17, verse 20):

> दातव्यमिनति यद्दानं दीयतेऽनुपकारिणे।
> देशे काले च पात्रे च तद्दानं सात्त्विकं स्मृतम्।।
> DATTAVYAMITI YADDANAM DEEYATENUPA-KARINE. DESHE KALE CHA, PATRE CHA TADDANAM SATTVIKAM SMARITAM

"That gift is made to one who can make no return, with the feeling that it is one's duty to give, and which is given at the right place and time and to a worthy person, that gift is held *satvik*".

Real charity is that which provides permanent supply of honest earning to the poor. Charities of all kinds are good but the best of them is that of imparting divine knowledge. The great law giver Manu says:

> सर्वेशर्मेव दानानांब्र:र्णदर्नविशिश्यत
> SARVESHARMEVA DANANAMBRAHRNADANAM VISHISHYAT

"Imparting of divine knowledge is the best of all charities". For it is through information that man achieves happiness during this world and salvation for himself. The *Gita* also says:

> अदेशकाले यद्दंपत्रेभ्यश्च देयते।
> असत्कृतर्नवजनार्तन तत्त्रनास्मुदाहृतम्।।
> "ADESHAKALE YADDAMAPATREBHYASCHA
> DEYATE ASATKRUTARNAVAJANATARN TATTAR-
> NASAMUDAHRUTAM"

The *Gita*, that is given at a wrong place or time to unworthy persons, without respect or with insult that is declared to *betamasika* (the worst type of gift). No charity with vanity—

> "शताहस्तसमहार, सहस्राहस्तसंकिकरा।"
> "SHATAHASTA SAMAHARA, SAHASRAHASTA SANKIRA"

"Earn with many hands, and distribute with thousands". (*Atharvaveda*, 3-24-5). It is also said, in relation to charity. "To live is to give. Gita as long as you live". Thus, *Sewa* is a continuous life long process.

Significance and Importance of *Sewa* in Life

"The best reasonably *Sewa* is one that avoids the expectation of any reward, return, name or fame, one that doesn't destroy the self-respect and confidence of sentiments of the beneficiary". Hindu philosophers have attached a very great importance to *sewa* as a selfless and loving service to others. *Sewa* occupies a high position in one's spiritual life and advancement. One mustn't solely look for to alleviate misery of his fellow-men however conjointly establish himself with them and become a vicinity of them thus on endure their suffering and share in their misery. "He alone lives who lives for the sake of serving to others" says the *Rig Veda*:

> परेशमुपकरूरथं यज्जिवतीसजीवती।
> Pareshamupakarurtham Yajjivatisajivati

This thought is exemplified within the story King Ranti Deva written by Sage Veda Vyasa. It so happened during his reign that his kingdom was gripped once by severe and devastating famine, his subjects were hungry and distressed. Moved by their suffering, the king determined that he would share in their misery and decided to fast himself until all the hungry were fed. His fast lasted for forty eight days throughout that amount he took no food and not even water however served his poor subjects. At the trip of forty eight days of fast, he wanted to break his fast by taking a morsel of food and a glass of water. His ministers and councillors were with him at the time of breaking his fast. Just when he was about to drink a glass of water, he heard the cry of Polkas asking for water to drink desperately. The King immediately ordered that his glass of water be passed on to Polkas in spite of the remonstrations of his ministers and his own condition. He then proceeded to eat a morsel of food. Just at that point a guest came at his door requesting food. The King gave all his food to the guest. The individuals around him pleaded with him to not do thus, since his life itself was at risk. The reply that the King gave at that time stands out because the attitude of the actuality *sewakarta* (server). He said:

> I don't look for from God the best seventh heaven attended with eight sorts of powers (suddhis). Nor do I look after my own salvation or freedom from the cycle of births and deaths. My only desire is to be present in all beings (share their feelings) and undergo suffering with them and serve them so that they may become free from misery, hunger, thirst, fatigue, loss of strength in limbs, distress, grief disappointment delusion—all these undesirable options of my distressed soul have all disappeared upon my giving water to at least one who was suffering from acute thirst. (Sewajyoti, 2019).

Dharma and Society: Repository of Social Life

The concept of *Dharma* in Hindu philosophy is of much significance as it is the life-line of the whole social life. *Dharma* concept carries a wider meaning and to explain it in a single definition acceptable in all contexts will be an effort in futile. What is intended in the following paras, is to highlight its meaning from social work point of views and to enumerate how social work was envisaged through the concept of *Dharma* in ancient Hindu literature.

The Dictionary meaning of the word *Dharma* includes, "Virtue, good work, duty, prescribed course of conduct" etc. But the Sanskrit terms are potent with deeper meaning than these English words. The word *Dharma* is derived from the Sanskrit root **Dhru** meaning to hold together, to preserve. "It is the norm which sustains the universe, the principle of a thing in virtue of which it is what it is". Shrikrishna says, *Dharma* is so called because it protects all. *Dharma* preserves all that is created and also *Dharma* is meant for the welfare of all. The purpose of *Dharma* is the well-being of all as Shrikrishna says, "*Dharma* is created for the well-being of all the living creatures". Again Swayambhuwa Brahma has created *Dharma* for the well-being of all and with the growth of *Dharma*, the growth and development of all take places. It is *Dharma* from which happiness and beatitude results. Shrikrishna says, "I take form for protecting the good destroying the evil for the purpose of establishing *Dharma*". Dr. Sinha notes, "*Dharma* is what is conducive to the welfare of all being which is the supreme duty; devotion to the highest good of humanity is the highest *Dharma*". In social principle, Manu conceives *Dharma* as the perfect social principle which helps the upholder. Explaining the consequences of destruction of *Dharma*, Manu says, "one who destroys *Dharma*; gets destroyed himself while *Dharma* protects him who upholds *Dharma*". Overall:

- *Dharma* is a comprehensive concept in which social work is taken care of.
- *Dharma* envisages the principles which have to be observed daily in the social relations with the purpose of welfare of all in one's mind.
- *Dharma* was the chief factor that shaped men's lives and the *Dharma* engrossed everyone for the welfare of others and be like friendly social workers in thoughts and deeds.
- *Dharma* as a social principle upholds the dignity of all and sustains the social life for its smooth functioning which helped the society to help itself. (Bhat, 2018)

Reform Movements and Hindu Sangathan

Hindu Nationalism acquired a significant push in the early twentieth century due to several socio-religious reformist and revivalist movements. Colonialism introduced several important developments to the India and missionary activity was one of them (Kaviraj, 1997, 330-31). These missionary activities were threats to indigenous culture. To combat these threats local communities adapted Western organizational models (Gold, 1994). Due to all these Hindu religious communities underwent a drastic transformation. It became gradually unified and homogenized from being "a juxtaposition of flexible religious sects" (Thapar, 1985) in the pre-colonial period. The colonial government tried to colour Hinduism as an orthodox and polytheistic religion. At the later part of nineteenth century, Hindu identity was witnessed through the formation of several groups of *sangathan* (organizations of patriotic men and their intention was to constitute a novel community to face the dominant character of Christianity. Service had always been more in the nature of personal charity in the Hindu Tradition in the form of idea of 'danapunya'. Thus, while *dana* was a deep-rooted 'living tradition' of Hinduism (Watt, 2005), it was metamorphosed to a more modern form of service that came to be defined as *sewa*. The *sewa* and reform activities really contributed in the creation of strong nationalism. *Yatras* and open celebration of festivals were the key factors in consolidation of Hindu. Previously, these activities came under private affairs. *Hindutva* was codified for the first time in 1923 when V.D. Savarkar laid down geographical, racial, and cultural criteria for Hinduness (Savarkar, 1969). Dr. K.B. Hedgewar founded the Rashtriya Swayamsevak Sangh in 1925 to promote a corporate and unified *hindurastra*. The RSS was influenced by Hindu Sangathans and retained their emphasis on *Sewa*. Under the patronage and sponsorship of the Rashtriya Swayamsevak Sangh and its *Parivar*, the concept of *Sewa* was arrayed for fortification of Hindu communities.

RSS: Redefining *Sewa*

The institution of *sewa* has been an integral part of the Rashtriya Swayamsevak Sangh since its formation (Beckerlegge, 2003, 40). Under Golwalkar's leadership, the Sangh formed the Hindu Sahayata Samiti that played a major role in organizing relief and protection for the Hindu refugees who were fleeing from East and West Pakistan (Kanungo, 2003, 55).

Nanaji Deshmukh: An Epitome of Social Service and Social Development

Nanaji Deshmukh could be a one that wants no introduction. His sharp intellect and extraordinary organizing skill has put an indelible mark in Indian politics. Born on October 11, 1916 in a modest Maharashtra family at Kadoli, a small town in Parbhani district, Nanaji had little money to pay for his tuition fees and books. Nanaji was deeply inspired by Lokamanya Tilak and his nationalist ideology. He showed keen interest in welfare work and activities. He established India's 1st Saraswati Sishu Mandir at Gorakhpur in 1950. Nanaji Deshmukh did a lot of social work in Gonda (U.P.) and Beed (Maharashtra). The motto of his project was: ***(Har hath ko denge kaam, har khet ko denge paanee).*** Nanaji devoted his entire time to Deendayal Research Institute that he himself established way back in 1969. During NDA government headed by Shri Atal Bihari Vajpyaee, Nanaji was nominated to Rajya Sabha in 1999 as recognition to his services to the nation. Nanaji died on 27 February, 2010.

Chitrakoot Project: Towards Self-reliance

Chitrakoot project is integrated and holistic model for Republic of India. Deendayal Upadhyaya conceptualized to create a society based on the complimentarity of the family, basic educational institute and the indigenous populace. The Chitrakoot project is a unique crusade that was launched on 26 January of 2002 and was likely to cover 500 villages around Chitrakoot in two phases. The 80 villages haunted within the first section was going to be autonomous by 15 August, 2005, and therefore the remaining villages can succeed independence by 26th January, 2009. The campaign has also been started in the villages covered by the institute in Gonda and Beed District. The self-containment crusade ensures all facts and facets of individual, family and societal life of the villagers. The main features of the crusade within the idea of Samaj Shilpi Dampati, 'graduate' couples that lives within the villages itself, and are accountable for inspiring and managing a cluster of five villages. The main purpose of Chitrakoot project is to focus on following points:

Agriculture

Our Krishi Vigyan Kendras are engaged in converting non-economic holdings into economic holdings. Poor farmers are creating all out effort to attain independent development. This will lead to surplus agriculture production in the villages. These 80 villages were now be able to supply their organic products to cities in limited amounts. In this way, self-reliant farmers will help in improving the health of urban citizens.

Education (Gurukul)

Deendayal Research Institute has established *Gurukuls* on the ancient *Gurukul* educational pattern. Children of all social strata can live and learn within the *Gurukul*. 10 *Gurukuls*, each with a capacity to house 20 students have been constructed. Six *Gurukuls* will be for boys while four will be for girls. 20 students will reside in one *Gurukul*, and to take care of them one retired couple will be there who will act as parents for these students, besides them two attendant will be there. In this way, the family of 24 members will be in one *Gurukul*. Each *Gurukul* is going to be having its own land wherever the scholars can cultivate vegetables for his or her utilization. One cow will also be there in each *Gurukul*. So, in this way, the students can get the nutritious milk. These *Gurukuls* can prove the centre for social unity and integrity. Besides the academic studies, the students will get the training in different trades in *Udyamita*. These are bamboo crafting, fruits and vegetables processing, bakery production, garments manufacturing, screen printings etc. so that they may become "self-reliant" since their childhood (Chitrakoot, 2019).

Health and Hygiene (Dadi Ma Ka Batua)

Traditionally, grandmothers in the family used to keep a medicinal pouch which use to contain various locally available medicines. She used them to cure several health disorders. There were treatments that evolved through experience. Arogyadham has prepared medicines prepared in its Rasashala used in this kit. All frequently occurring diseases can be treated by these medicines. All these medicines are prepared through regionally obtainable herbs.

Socially aware persons within the villages have additionally been trained within the use of those medicines. They treat the patients in the village. Chronic and serious patients are sent to Arogyadham at Chitrakoot for further treatment (Chitrakoot, 2019).

Entrepreneurship Development (Udyamita Vidyapeeth)

To achieve the goal of "Self- Reliance", Deendayal Research Institute has established Industrial training facilities for men and women of the Chitrakoot region. In Udyamita Vidyapeeth, the assorted sheds are established wherever ideal rural youth of the villages return and acquire the coaching in their interested field. After getting the training try to go their own place and start their own work in the village, in this way the unemployed rural youth are becoming the entrepreneur. At present, the trainings on the subsequent measure being provided in Udyamita Vidyapeeth viz. Fruits & vegetable processing, Oil expeller unit, Readymade garments, Screen & offset printing, M.C.R. tiles, Flour Mill, Cane and Bamboo craft and Computer training etc.

Models for Rural Development

Talking about the country as a whole, roughly two third of our people still live in villages. Their average income is only about half of the average income of their urban counterparts. Creating conditions to raise their income to become comparable or better than what is possible in urban areas is in my view the critical challenge before our education and development programs. The education while it contributes to development of capable human resource could also create new inputs for our society as well as our industry through:

- New innovations based on latest knowledge acquisitions ahead of others. This would create a superior edge for our country in terms of new products and processes giving us a competitive edge in the local as well as global market,
- Linking knowledge institutions to ongoing socio-economic activities in business/industrial entities to overcome obsolescence issues and maintain/regain their competitiveness, and
- Exploring issues of development or nearer to the base of socio-economic pyramid and devise as well as implement solutions to minimize disparities in our society.

Linking education and development this way would significantly enrich higher education while at the same time paving the way for development on a more sound footing in a bottom up mode. A typical framework to pursue such an approach, is to set up what I call a CILLAGE (city in a village), a knowledge centre within a rural domain with modern research activities and living facilities to attract capable researchers.

Such initiative or model like Mahatma Gandhi Chitrakoot Gramodaya Vishwavidyalaya demonstrates that self-reliance could be possible. The neighbourhood could learn through this type of successful enterprise.

RHRDF is beneficial for the neighbourhood through knowledge, skill and capacity building but also the institution hosting it through exposure of students and faculty to real life challenges enriching the learning process and facilitating greater relevance and impact of research being carried out through choice of research problems that people in the neighbourhood want to be solved. In addition to upholding technology enabled development and related gain in terms of livelihood enhancement, a city in the village can also add to a new model in the school education around (Kakodkar, 2016).

Role of Nanaji Deshmukh in Bhoodan Movement

Our modern Rishi, Nanaji Deshmukh has delicately participated in Bhoodan Movement. Basically the Bhoodan movement or land Gift movement was a voluntary land reform movement in India. It was initiated by Archarya Vinoba Bhave in 1951 at Pochampally village, which is how in Telangana, and known as Bhoodan Pochampally. Landless labourers got tiny plots on that they were welcome to settle and grow their crops. Bhoodan Acts were passed that expressed that the beneficiary had no right to sell the land or use it for non-agricultural functions. He was followed by crowds nearly all over he went. This movement developed into a village gift or *gramdan* movement. The movement lost its pace by the end of 1960. The Sarvodaya Samaj failed to build the mass movement that will ignite pressure for social transformation. Though, the movement somehow contributed in other way like public moral responsibilities and creating pressure on property owners. The entire scenario felt in favour of landless (Study.com, 2019).

Integral Humanism and Self-Reliance

Deendayal Upadhayay's foresight that much of what he suggested fifty years ago may see unsurprising to many since it is now part of the established discourse of *Bharatiyata* thoughts. His lectures on Integral Humanism sought-after to look at existing socio-political and economic ideas and systems and posit an alternate mode of living supported the traditions of *Sanatan Dharma*. Deendayal Upadhyaya considers Hindu deity the overarching principle that ought to govern all social, political and private life. Upadhyaya associates the preponderance of power, including economic monopolies, as a source of corrupt and *adharmic* misconduct. In his lecture, Deendayal Upadhyaya discusses the dynamics of how societies form and function. He disputes the notion that society is the summation of its individuals, created by some sort of social contract. He asserts that, "Nations don't acquire existence by a mere cohabitation". Society, in the view of Upadhyaya, has an autonomous ontology and is not necessarily coterminous with geographical space. He makes a noteworthy distinction between personal moralities which arises from social dynamics. He recognizes that individuals, who are moral in their personal life, can be immoral in their behaviour towards society and *vice versa*.

Deendayal Upadhyaya defines the nation as more substantial than the individuals comprising it, deriving from an ideal connected to a motherland and, presumably, its culture and historic memories. The values that represent the state he defines as 'Chiti', commendable attributes recognized as meritorious. He almost posits an *a priori* constitutive morality for personhood. To elaborate: "Chiti is that the criterion on that every action, each attitude is tested, and determined to be acceptable or otherwise. 'Chiti' is the soul of the nation. On the strength of this 'Chiti', a nation arises, strong and virile if it is this 'Chiti' that is demonstrated in the actions of every great man of a nation."

Upadhyaya makes the interesting point that historic Hindu society survived and continued to function because it was not synonymous with State organization though also calamitously affected by the capture of their State by invaders: "Those nations, whose life centred within the state, were finished with the end of the state. On the opposite hand, where state was not believed central to its life, the nation survived the transfer of political power." The characteristic of the resilience of self-governing Hindu communities, identified by Deendayal Upadhyaya, may be contrasted with the collapse of Buddhist communities in past centuries. Power in Buddhist communities was centralized and lower levels of organization dependent on State patronage from above in order to function. In the aftermath of foreign conquest, collapse radiated to all levels quickly (Sen, 2016). However, Upadhyaya additionally recognizes the importance of the State, which historical Hindu society, sturdy at alternation levels, could have not reinforce sufficiently, a doable reason for it succumbing to invaders. "*Dharma* wields its own power. *Dharma* is important in life. Shri Ramdas would further have preached to Shivaji to become a mendicant and unfold *Dharma* following his own example. But on the contrary, he galvanized Shivaji to increase his rule, as a result of state too, is a crucial establishment of the society." At the constant time, *Dharma*, consistent with Upadhyaya, is not confined to places of worship, neither is it substitutable with faith. He argues, it is much broader, the basis for sustaining society and the universe itself, varying in time and place, depending on circumstances and need.

References

Abhyankar, P. (2019). *Sewa Disha: Prelude*. P-9, RSB, Delhi, pp. 0-9.

About Sewa. (2019, September 27). Retrieved from https://sewauyk.org/&ved.

Bhagwat, M. (2019). *Sewa Disha: Sewa is awaking the simhatva feeling in the society*, p. 21, RSS, RSB, Delhi, pp. 21-24.

Bhat, N. (2018). *Social work in ancient Hindu literature*, pp. 56-59 Sheshadri Sadan, Tulsibag Road, Mahal, Nagpur: Bhartiya Shikshan Mandal.

Bhoodan Movement: Development & Mission. (2019, October 2). Retrieved from https://study.com/academy/lesson/bhoodan-movement-development-mission.html&ved.

Chitrakoot project. (2019, September 14). Retrieved from https://www.chitrakoot.org/&ved.

Goswami, D. (2011). *Bhagavad Gita*-17.20, p. 207, Gita Press, Gorakhpur.

Hiremath, S. (2010). *Parivartan: Serve Man-Serve Bhagwan*. RSB, Delhi: Rashtriya Sewa Bharti.

Joshi, S. (2019). *Sewa Disha: The best medium of transformation*, p. 11, RSB, Delhi.

Kakodkar, A. (2016). *Cillage: Revisiting S&T INSPIRED Indian model of holistic development*. Retrieved from http://www.anilkakodkar.in/presentations/lectures/Nanaji-memorial-lercture.pdf&ved.

Kanungo, Pralay, (2003). *RSS's Tryst with Politics: From Hedgewar to Sudarshan*. New Delhi: Manohar.

Kaviraj, Sudipta. (1997). *Religion and identity in India. Ethnic and Racial Studies*, 2: 325-44.

Sewajyoti's social commitments. (2019, September 10). Retrieved from https://Sewajyoti.com/news/about/us/conceptofsewa/&ved.

Sewa in your daily life. (2019, September 27). Retrieved from https://yogamour.org/letters-from-the-heart/2014/5/29/five-ways-to-practice-sewa-in-your-life&ved.

Sen, G. (2019). *Integral Humanism of Deendayal Upadhyaya*. Retrieved from http://spmrf.org/wp-content/uploads/2016/01/occasional-paper.pdf&ved.

ewa. (2019, September 14). Retrieved from https://www.yogapedia.com/definition/4999/Sewa.

ıvarkar, Vinayak Damodar (1969) *Hindutva: Who is a Hindu?* Bombay.

The nature of human life. (2019, September 14). Retrieved from https://www.bbc.couk/bitesize/guides/zmcf3k7/revision/3&ved.

Thapar, Romila (1985). *Syndicated Moksha*. Seminargli: 14-22.

Watt, Carey Anthony (2005). *Serving the Nation: Culture of Service, Association, and Citizenship in Colonial India*. New Delhi: Oxford University Press.

10

Integral Humanism and Social Work

Nipun Savarna and *Amod Gurar*

Introduction

Social work is one of the few professions where the aim is to resurrect the social cohesion whenever it is shaken by any turbulence. Every society is peculiar in its nature and to work with every society, social worker has to develop need based strategies using local knowledge, trends and theories which are according to the society and its need or else instead of strengthening the cohesion the social workers will make the situation even worse. But ironically in India, we have completely neglected the part of the definition of social work by IFSW which suggest "underpinned by theories of social science, humanities and ***indigenous knowledge*** we have blindly adopted the Western knowledge and created an agglomeration of the syllabus where most of the part of it remain limited to the books only and won't be applicable in Indian scenario. It is not that we don't have to adapt these theories, but we need a better option to work with the Indian plethora.

When talking about developing an indigenous structure of social work, the concept of INTEGRAL HUMANISM can be poll bearer in the process of Indianization and there is no question on this concept as it is locally developed one and which binds the Indian society. While most of the theories of social work at present differentiate the society, the concept of integral humanism holistically talks about binding the society in one thread and integrate each component of the society.

Integral Humanism and Social Work

The concept of integral humanism was first introduced by Pandit Deendayal Upadhyaya, in the form of four lectures delivered in Bombay on April 22-25, 1965. In a nutshell, the concept of integral humanism advocates integrating all the good component of the Western knowledge along with the Indic knowledge and hence creating a cluster of philosophy that can guide towards the rejuvenation of the country.

During the pre-1947 era-focus of the countrymen was on liberating India from the alien rule which hijacked the country for more than 700 years (including Mughals, British and others). But after the independence, the question was about what model should be adopted to guide new India and to fight different kinds of evil existing in the country till now. Although we had people like M.K. Gandhi (Hind Swaraj), Lokmanya Tilak (Gita Rahasya) which presented some impeccable work which included Indic approach but neglecting all these ideas and following philosophy of west is best we blindly adopted alien theories of socialism without having proper debate on the concept and its relevance for the Indian context.

Originated in the west not only these thoughts and philosophies were alien to our country but also were developed according to the needs of Indian society and European view in mind. Panditji in his lecture said:

> "A nation wishes to remain independent so that, they can progress according to their natural bent and can experience happiness in their endeavour. Nature is powerful and an attempt to disgrace her leads to trouble. The natural instinct cannot be disgraced but it is possible to elevate this nature to the level of culture". Upadhyaya, 1965 (avap.org.in).

Keeping the chaos created by these alien concepts Panditji presented a view known as Integral Humanism, where he provided a direction by advocating a holistic approach of dealing with the problems rather than dealing with a particular fragment to solve the problem. He relied heavily on Indic root and then picking good elements from the Western concepts.

Integral Humanism and its Relevance in Social Work

Social work is a boon to society because it is what makes us human a social being and generates a sense of cohesiveness within the human beings and provides the human in any kind of social turbulence with the option of getting help from trained professionals. But when the professional lacks the local knowledge it becomes tough for not only the professional to perform the task but also it becomes tough for the locals to accept the methods practiced by the workers. Our course promotes the concept of Marxism, socialism, liberalism, etc. It's not that these concepts are absurd but it's simply alien to our society and will create more chaos instead of binding it. Dealing with the social problems of our country with European knowledge is like providing a headache patient remedy for stomach ache.

Here integral humanism as an Indic concept can pave way for the process of indigenization.

Integral Humanism's philosophy can be a pioneer in the accomplishment of the goal of social cohesiveness. While most of the Western philosophies like Capitalism (which made a freely working labour 'servant' of capitalists), Communalism (which always talks about bloodshed) and other isms which divides society in fragments and creates a sense of hatred, the integral humanism advocates holistically dealing with the issues where social cohesiveness is at stake. It not only focuses on empowering the weak but also the aim is to make the strong realize their responsibility towards making it sure that in such conditions whenever evident he/she should voluntarily be the flag bearer of making the weak strong again and there should be no need of a particular policy to help them. And also this idea will increase a sense of social cohesiveness.

Also, most of the time the ecosystem of Western knowledge talks about the concept of AAZADI (freedom) in social work and this system sounds absurd in this case. Because the gregarious nature of human beings and the concept of human beings being free is also very absurd. Since our birth, we human beings are dependent on our fellow human beings and hence we are stranded in a web of relationship and hence our focus should not be on freedom but on a better synchronization. And that is what the concept of Integral humanism advocates this thing.

Not only social cohesiveness but taking inspiration from the notion of *vasudhaiva kutumbakam* this theory of integral humanism advocates the notion of kinship instead of equality. Equality is something which is nothing but a mere utopia because it can't be achieved at every front like economic, mental etc. However, a sense of unity can be incorporated within the mind of people by following the principle of kinship so that we have hands surrounding us to help.

In India, the philosophy has been the key to success of Indian growth and glory during ancient times. While in West philosophy was not having a firm grip over the school of thoughts, in India this very philosophy was treated as an independent subject and since ages has guided many scientists or thinkers. It was the master key for all the complex studies. That's why the Indian knowledge system was so much fruitful and successful in achieving its goal. (Radhakrishnan, 1923).

Our rich cultural roots and their importance in society can be understood with analysis of the way Hindu temples of our society used to function. The temple during ancient India were not just a mere place to perform *Yajna* but were associated with a lot of services related to social welfare. The temples used to receive a lot of donation and each member of the society used to donate something—be it wealth or foodgrains as per their capacities. The wealth of the temple thus generated was used to carry out a number of social services ranging from providing free education to the students to providing shelter to refugee. The services provided by the temples were diverse and the role played by temples in building society's harmony very important. Indeed, these days also there are foundations like Akshaypatra Foundation of ISKCON and Shirdi temple which is performing a similar kind of works these days, but the scale is very low (Balakrishna, 2018). There are many examples from history where we can find the ancient tradition of the country paving way for amalgamation of different segments of society if we study, the beautiful tree by Shri Dharampal we will find out how *Gurukul* system was paving a way for providing free education to the different segments of the society. When these ancient traditions and philosophies will be used to create a theory for the social work curriculum it will not only be a more synchronized one as per Indian society but also it will provide a better path for development of the Indian society (Dharampal, 1983).

One of the examples of social service which has been evolved from the *Bharatiya* ideology is that of Langar provided at *gurudwara*, following the concept of *Niswarth Sewa*, Sikhs have been providing food to every person irrespective of their religion, caste or colour. This concept of *langar* is an example of dealing with the issue of hunger holistically rather than limiting it for a particular group of people because you never know who out of a plethora of people dwelling around the streets is hungry. Often the social remedies provided according to Western philosophy are focused on individualistic approach which although provides the solution but is quite limited in nature defying the very basic nature of the human society that is gregariousness. While the problem of individuals should be dealt with individually but applying this individualistic approach to solve the issue of a community will lead to chaos and instead of achieving the basic goal of social cohesion all we could achieve is social disintegration.

It's not that Indian society was free of flaws, there were flaws in Indian society but the way these flaws were handled were more Indian in nature rather than blindly adopting a philosophy that was alien to the land. It can be understood with the example of the Gandhian approach of integrating Indian society. One of the key aspects of Gandhian movement was that he relied on linking the different aspects of Indian social upliftment with common people of India, be it the notion of *Satyagraha* or *Asahyoga*. Gandhi took his inspiration from the very root of the country because in a country like India if you have to make people understand a point then you must use techniques which are synchronized with the lifestyle of the millennium and can jolt them emotionally. Gandhi somehow mastered this trick. Gandhi took his inspiration from *Bhagwat Geeta* as mentioned by Gandhians. *Bhagwat Geeta* in itself is an ocean, Many scholars have often argued that this text holds the solution to every problem a human can encounter during his/her lifetime. For Gandhi, the notion of an ideal society was *Ramrajya* as mentioned in *Shri*

Ramcharitamanas. *Ramrajya* was the most ideal form of society where each and every word was counted and was more holistic. Gandhi during his entire movement acknowledged this fact and imagined the Indian state following the philosophy. Expressing his idea about the notion of an ideal society for India, Gandhi wrote—

"'BY RAMARAJYA' I do not mean Hindu Raj. I mean by Ramarajya Divine Raj, the Kingdom of God. For me, Rama and Rahim are one and the same deity. I acknowledge no other God but the one God of truth and righteousness.

Whether Rama of my imagination ever lived or not on this earth, the ancient ideal of Ramarajya is undoubtedly one of true democracy in which the meanest citizen could be sure of swift justice without an elaborate and costly procedure. Even the dog is described by the poet to have received justice under Ramarajya". (Gandhi, 1929).

It was the rich heritage of ours which since ages had been a source of inspiration of social reformists like Gandhi but still when it came to producing a bunch of social worker for India we failed to acknowledge the fact and despite the fact that Gandhian philosophy has inspired persons like Nelson Mandela and Martin Luther King *Junior the Indian root was neglected*. Thanks to the love of Indian intellectuals for white's ecstasy.

Indeed, one of the key advocacies of social work is the democratic rights of individual and this was since ages have been part of our folk stories. In *Ramayana*, the concept of *Ramrajya* shows a splendid example of how democracy works where even the voice of a washerman was noticed. While we may have a debate on whether this decision was good or not, the fact is that we cannot deny the fact that it was an example of how an ideal democracy should work, a state where even most minor voice was heard and not only heard but acknowledged, a practice that can't be observed in modern-day democracy. Not only *Ramayana* but events from history like Lichhvi empire was one of the first democracy in this world. Here also the Indian philosophy has been a pioneer.

There are numerous events in Indian roots be it at the level of philosophy or at the level of practice where the Indian ideology, when inculcated with the social work, can act as a lighthouse to guide the social worker to work flawlessly in Ocean of Indian society.

Another example depicting the rich resource of our own culture is the way animals were treated in Indian stories or culture. While acknowledging nature has been a very recent development in social work when the workers started talking about the rights of animals, Indian folk stories have been worshipping animals for ages. Indeed, according to the Indic style of governance an ideal Kingdom is the one where even rights of animals are acknowledged.

The Western knowledge system in social work usually has a preset theory and philosophy. Now while it may work flawlessly in Western society owing to the homogenous nature of the society but in India, such a system turns out to be shallow. There is a proverb in India that in this country even language changes after every 12 miles, now in a country having such a diverse population the theories need revision. In our country, the treatment should be designed according to the area owing to the heterogeneous nature of Indian society. Another problem which social workers have been encountering while working in Indian society is related to the sensitive nature of Indian society. Indian society is very delicate if we simply apply a method of social work without acknowledging the heterogeneous and sensitive nature of Indian society we will end up disintegrating the society instead of increasing the social cohesiveness. And in situation like these, the concept of integral humanism can be a boon. Be it Gandhi, Vivekananda or other Indian social reformers their movement against social evils were successful because they for the purpose of social upliftment and their fight against social evils relied more upon the area specific measures and by acknowledging the heterogenous nature of the Indian society they achieved huge success.

The above-mentioned examples show us the strong foundation we already have to design a method of practice which is more effective for working in Indian society. When we will use our knowledge along with the modern social philosophy we will develop a strong foundation for working in Indian set up.

These fragments are just few of the components from the unfathomable ocean of integral humanism. The concept displays the sheer brilliance of our Indic concept and how we can utilize it to deal with the social problems of India. Like our body where all organs work in a synchronized and systematic manner to form organ system and similarly organ system work to form our body. Our society and individual like this should work similarly.

Conclusion

While there has been discussion going on about Indianization of the social work course in the country, the quest has been started to develop theories and practice method which can act like a lighthouse to guide the ships sailing towards the accomplishment of this goal. As mentioned above, the solution to social problems of India has been already present in the very root of Indian culture. It's not that we advocate to completely neglect the Western knowledge system but we must acknowledge the Indian roots while designing the new course where an amalgamation of Western knowledge guided by Indian philosophy should be created which would be the best system for the practice of social work in India. And in a nutshell that's what Pandit Deendayal was advocating when he first coined the concept of Integral Humanism. The concept was all about integrating all the gems of knowledge and putting them together to create a system that will make India Great again and in context of social work education, this is all about acknowledging the Indian philosophy.

References

Balakrishna, S. (2018). *70 Years of Secularism*, Indus University.

Dharmpal, D. (1983). *The beautiful tree: Indigenous Indian Education in the eighteenth Century*. Other India Press.

Gandhi, M. (1929), *Ramrajya*, retrieved from https://www.mkgandhi.org/momgandhi/chap67.htm

Pandit Deen Dayal Upadhyay (April 22-25, 1965). *Integral Humanism*, retrieved from. http://avap.org.in/Uploads/Publication/Integral%20 Humanism3.pdf

Radhakrishnan, S. (1923), *Indian Philosophy*, Vol. 1. The Macmillan Company.

Sharma, M.C. (2018), *Integral Humanism: An analysis of some basic elements*, Prabhat Prakashan.

11

Nanaji

As a Paragon of Service in the District of Chitrakoot

P.K. Tripathi and *M. Dwivedi*

Chitrakoot, veritably, is the heart of India. This is not merely due to its geographical area. This is so because Lord Ram reigns supreme in the heart of people. In current scenario of lust for power, this is the only place of inspiration where Shri Ram and Bharat showed that attainment of political power does not lead to the achievement of greatness. Greatness comes from dedicated services for the people. Reviving this spirit in present and future generations, who are the builder of nation, there is no better place than Chitrakoot to start a revolution.[1]

With this consideration Nanaji (as a social activist) started "Gramodaya" (rural reconstruction) initiatives in the District Chitrakoot where he has made a lot of contributions in the field of rural self-reliance, education and health to promote villager's life. Nanaji's life is a mission and his mission is his life. He made up his mind while he is in school to dedicate his life for the service of motherland. During his whole life, he stood as a paragon for millions of people who came to his contact through different programmes. He implemented the philosophy of integral humanism to improve the living standard of more than 150 villages and did pioneering work towards the anti-poverty and minimum needs. He was also instrumental in carrying out social restructuring programme in over 50 hundred villages of both Uttar Pradesh and Madhya Pradesh state of India. He did a lot of social work in Gonda and Beed—the most backward districts of Uttar Pradesh and Maharashtra states of India. He was inspired by Lokmanya Tilak and his nationalist ideology. Later, he settled in Chitrakoot, a holy place on the border of Uttar Pradesh and Madhya Pradesh states and made Chitrakoot the centre of his social activities. He established first Rural University of India named as Mahatma Gandhi Chitrakoot Gramodaya Vishwavidyalaya formerly Chitrakoot Gramodaya Vishwavidyalaya. Nanaji developed a model for the development of rural area on the basis of integral humanism. The basis of this project is overall transformation through overall development with people's initiatives and participation. He believes in the concept of health is wealth. Good health is a real power of human body which increases positive capacity to perform various activities so that Nanaji focused on health with establishment of Arogyadham in the district Chitrakoot. He also relied on Mahatma Gandhi's ideal concept of self-reliant village communities. Since villagers' income is almost dependent on agriculture, so he worked to develop agricultural sector to make them self-reliant. With this vision, he established Deen Dayal Research Institute in Chitrakoot. All these social activities of Nanaji contributed to both economic and moral upliftment of rural India, towards achieving the idea of Ram Rajya.

Deen Dayal Research Institute (DRI)

Deen Dayal Research Institute (DRI), set-up on March 8, 1968 under the inspirational guidance of Bharat Ratna Shri Nanaji Deshmukh, which works in the philosophy of "Integral Humanism". It offers different services in rural areas which include health, hygiene, education, training for self-employment etc. to achieve overall socio-economic development of individuals of Rural Indian society. The developmental programmes under DRI have been carried out at various centres viz. Delhi, Gonda, Balrampur (U.P.), Chitrakoot (U.P. & M.P.), Beed, Nagpur (Maharashtra). The mission statement of Deendayal Research Institute is 'We are not for ourselves but for our kith and kins are those who are oppressed and neglected" (DRI, 2019).

The objectives of DRI are as follows:

- To carry out research in Social Science with a view to reconstruct Indian Society.

- To establish Rural Development and Training centres for carrying out research with a view to motivate people in adopting new and improved technologies in the field of sustainable Agriculture, Water Conservation and Alternative Industrialization and promote self-employment.
- Activities in the field of medical research, medical care, life-long health and medical education.
- To set-up Academic and Technical Vocational Training centres in rural areas.
- To eradicate social evils by propagating human values with the active cooperation and initiative of the people.
- To establish Dispute free Society.
- Integrated Tribal Development.
- To ensure people initiative and their active participation in various activities and programmes.
- To organize Intellectual Activities.
- To share the experience and Intellectual property with other Organizations (DRI, 2019).

The objectives of DRI were laid down by Nanaji, aiming at complete independence of villages and villagers in different areas such as agriculture, water resources, health, moral character, education and employment. Nanaji wanted to design a system of development based on local knowledge and technology to enhance the livelihood of the locals in spite of inviting external investments. However, there are challenges and the primary challenge was to win villagers' trust so that they are mentally prepared for the change. The secondary challenge was that there are minimum resources which require maximum efforts. As a pioneering step, the primary focus was on making agriculture a profitable venture because only prosperity can make a happy life and society and to achieve prosperity each and every person whether men, women or children have to contribute towards making agriculture a profitable venture. Initially in the district of Chitrakoot there was insufficient water supply which is very much important for agriculture. To resolve this problem, dams were constructed and this experiment has recharged the entire groundwater system around Chitrakoot.[2]

Education and University

In his days as a Pracharak, Nanaji established the first Saraswati Shishu Mandir in Gorakhpur. In Chitrakoot, he ensured that students not only get good education but also they become responsible citizens who earn a happy living and contribute to the integral development of a happy human race and not just become money-making machines which work only under the pressure. With this concept the Nanhi Duniya or the 'little world' pre-primary education begins where children of the age group of 3 to 5 years come to experience nature and not for study. At this pre-primary level they play with colours, balloons, models, maps and toys, and learn by interaction without reading and writing. Nanhi Duniya is a place for little children where they learn while playing with nature and interactive world. Primary education in Chitrakoot begins at Surendra Pal Vidyalaya where the children study standard curriculum. For post-secondary education, Nanaji founded the first Rural University in Chitrakoot district in Uttar Pradesh state of India known as the Mahatma Gandhi Chitrakoot Gramodaya Vishwavidyalaya. This university is well furnished with courses and equipments, including a fully equipped Geographical Information System Lab in its Geology department. All these educational steps inculcate cultural and moral values in children by relevant productive activities, self-reliance and holistic way of life.[2, 3]

Health and Hospital

Nanaji also believed that a society can be prosperous only when each and every individual of the society has good health. With this concept there came into existence the Aarogya Dhaam, that focuses on serving through *Ayurveda*, naturopathy and *yoga* which is a world class research centre as well as comprehensive health care centre. "The Arogya Dham campus, spread over 43 acres on the banks of the Mandakini river in Chitrakoot, aims at providing a model for the realization of a new life system, by taking a total overview of human development with *Yoga*, Naturopathy and *Ayurveda*. As the objective is to study the impact of parentage, family background, environment, upbringing, as well as the properties and effects of *Yoga* and *Ayurveda* on a life".[4] There exist different components of Aarogya Dhaam such as "Ayurveda Sadan (for Ayurvedic treatments and research), Ras Shala (where locally grown herbs are used for preparing ayuvedic medicines), Nidan Sadan (Out-Patients Department), Yoga Sadan (for yogic cure and training), Swasthya Kutir (health cottages that offer five star facilities with programmes for healthy physical, mental and emotional recovery), Matri Sadan (maternity and paediatric unit), Swasthya Sadan (In-Patients Department), a fully furnished dental unit, Aahar Vihar Sadan (canteen), a spawning herbal garden spreading many acres, and a large library and documentation centre."[4] This Arogyadhaam is surrounded by forests. This health centre clearly aims to cure a suffering body in all the possible ways such as mentally, emotionally, spiritually and physically and bring a total recovery of the whole body, heart and soul by totally using natural herbs and healing the entire human system. With the coordination of Arogyadham, DRI has also developed local herbal medicines and these local herbal medicines have been found to be very effective too and these local herbal medicines are famous as 'Dadi Maa Ka Batua'. This Dadi Maa Ka Batua kit has gained immense popularity in rural areas and has also helped and saved the villagers' life from different ailments and also relax them from expensive treatment and medicines.[2, 4]

Rural Self-Reliance and *Udyamita*

For the concept of rural self-reliance Udyamita Vidyapeeth has been established by Nanaji in district Chitrakoot which aims to change rural youth by motivational camps, awareness campaign, rural youth sammelans, rural youth committee, managing self help groups, training for the improvement of the skills such as traditional artisans, skill development programmes and entrepreneurship. Here youth in the age group of 18 to 35 years are catered. The initial step in this centre is to identify the interest of the rural youth to adopt self employment as per his interest. This is done by interface with experts and counselling in camps in rural areas which provides the Udyamita centre a valuable clue towards the capacity and ability of the rural youth. In this centre training of youth for self-employment is also emphasized to acquire different technical skills. At the centre 'learning by doing and learning by seeing' is followed which increases self-confidence in youths and also help the youths to increase their potential. Different skill programmes include bamboo crafts, motor driving, radio and TV repairing, tailoring and fashion designing, two wheeler repairs, bakery products, fruit and vegetable preservation, etc. In the sector of information technology IT-based training programmes have also been introduced for which a well established computer lab is also there.[5]

Nanaji's Life and His Efforts towards the Reconstruction of Society

Nanaji was born in Marathi Brahmin family at small town Kadoli in the Hingoli district on 11 October, 1916. He did the work of selling vegetables to raise money for his education. He completed high school from Sikar and achieved scholarship from Rao Raja of Sikar. Nanaji studied in Birla College where he connected with activities of Rashtriya Swayamsewak Sangh. Nanaji's birthplace was Maharashtra but he started his social activities in Rajasthan and Uttar Pradesh. After seeing the love and affection for motherland, RSS chief (Sar Sangh Chalak) Madhav Rao Sadashiv Rao Golwarkar sent him Uttar Pradesh. Nanaji also got inspired by Bal Gangadhar Tilak and his nationalist ideology. He was very much interested in social services and social activities. Besides that his family was very close to Keshav Ram Baliram Hedgewar family who frequently visits Deshmukh's family. He encouraged Nanaji to attend Sangh Shakha. After Keshav Ram Baliram Hedgewar's death in 1940, many youth joined the RSS in Maharashtra. Nanaji also joined RSS and since then devoted his entire life to the service of the nation. He was sent as a Pracharak to Agra, Uttar Pradesh where he met Pt. Deen Dayal Upadhyay. After which he was sent as a Pracharak to Gorakhpur where he faced a lot of difficulties to establish the Sangh ideology in east UP. At that time Sangh was having financial crunch. It had no fund, for serving daily needs of pracharaks. It was quite difficult task to manage due to lack of funds. Ultimately Baba Raghav Das had given shelter on this condition that he would also cook meals for him. After three years Nanaji's hard work got success and almost 250 Sangh Shakha were established around the Gorakhpur. Nanaji always focussed on education and hence he established India's first Saraswati Shishu Mandir at Gorakhpur in 1950. In those days, the Sangh decided that it would publish daily newspaper and Nanaji was assigned Managing Director of the newspaper along with Pt. Deen Dayal Upadhyay. At that time it was very difficult for publishing house to raise funds for publication. After the assassination of Mahatma Gandhi, the Sangh was banned and publication work was also interrupted but Nanaji continued the work of publication despite being underground. After lifting of the ban, Bharatiya Jan Sangh political party was formed. BJS got strength through Deen Dayal's vision in Uttar Pradesh with oratory skills of Atal Bihari Vajpayee and organizational work of Nanaji Deshmukh who started their important role in the state politics. Nanaji always established healthy relations not only with his party workers but also with his opponents also. The cordial relation of Nanaji Deshmukh with Dr. Ram Manohar Lohia changed the nature of Indian politics. Once Nanaji invited Ram Manohar Lohia in BJS worker's meeting where Lohia met with Pt. Deen Dayal Upadhyay and this association brought the BJS closer to other socialist leaders against the Congress government policies. Thus, Nanaji was not only worker of RSS and political face of BJS but also he was very active in Social Work. He played an important role with Vinoba Bhave and actively participated in "Bhoodan movement". Nanaji was also offered for Cabinet portfolio of industry during Janta Party Government. After revocation of the emergency, Nanaji had won the election from Balrampur Constituency of Uttar Pradesh. He was also nominated to Rajya Sabha by the NDA Government in the year 1999 in recognition of his contribution to the Nation. After moving from active politics, Nanaji established a social organization in 1969 which was named Deen Dayal Research Institute (DRI). He conributed a lot towards the poverty alleviation and minimum needs. The other area of his work was agriculture and cottage, rural education and health. Nanaji was chairman of DRI. He devoted all his time to work for this organization. Nanaji had given his contribution to run the social restructuring programmes over the 500 villages both Uttar Pradesh and Madhya Pradesh states of

India. He also worked for publication of journal "Manthan" which was edited by K.R. Malkani for many years. Nanaji spent his lots of time in Social Work. He did Social Work in different parts of India, like Gonda (UP), Balrampur and Beed (Maharashtra). He also established India's first rural University named as Chitrakoot Gramodaya Vishwavidyalaya where he served as Chancellor. He was pioneer of integral humanism philosophy for improving the quality of life of more than 150 villages of Bundelkhand. In the last stage of his life he was unhealthy due to geriatric problems and had refused shifting to Delhi for treatment. He donated his body to AIIMS for medical research through Dadhich Deh Daan Sanstha, New Delhi.[6, 7, 8] He was awarded Bharat Ratna in 2019 (posthumously) and Padma Vibhushan in 1999.

Conclusion

Definitely Nanaji was a great social activist of nineteenth century. As a social activist his services played an important role in different areas of the society well-being of the people. He was a national epitome of Indian Social Work. Nanaji contributed his whole life for upliftment of deprived and downtrodden people. There is no doubt that he was totally inspired from Pt. Deen Dayal Upadhyaya so he did his work towards 'Antyodaya via Gramodaya'. Because of his devotion as a social activist Government of India posthumously awarded him with Bharat Ratna (2019) which is the highest civilian award.

[**Acknowledgements :** We would like to thank Dr. Ajay Chourey, Associate Professor, Department of Social Work, Mahatma Gandhi Chitrakoot Gramodaya Vishwavidyalaya, Chitrakoot for providing all the required material and suggestions for improving the paper. I extend my gratitude to Dr. Bishnu Mohan Dash, Department of Social Work, B.R. Ambedkar College, University of Delhi, for continuously motivating us for the paper.]

Notes

1. http://www.chitrakoot.org/driindia/home.html retrieved on 25/12/2019.
2. https://arisebharat.com/2009/09/29/nanaji-makes-gramswaraj-a-reality retrieved on 25/12/2019.
3. Magazine, Chitrakoot Gramodaya Vishwavidyalaya: vision and action, 1999, University Publication, Chitrakoot.
4. http://www.chitrakoot.org/html/arogyadham.htm retrieved on 28/12/2019.
5. http://chitrakoot.org/driindia/udyamitavidyapeet.html retrieved on 28/12/2019.
6. Chauhan, G. (2005), *Nanaji Deshmukh Jivan Darshan*, Amar Satya Prakashan, New Delhi.
7. Kumar, R. (2019), *Bharat Ratn Nanaji Deshmukh*, Diamond Pocket Books, New Delhi.
8. Swaroop, D. (2017), *Rashtra Rishi Nanaji Deshmukh*, Prabhat Prakashan, Delhi.

12

Nanaji Deshmukh's Approach towards Community Development

Surender Verma and *Sunil Prasad*

Introduction

Nanaji Deshmukh was one of the three persons who were awarded Bharat Ratna in 2019. His contribution in the field of social work demands to declare his birth anniversary as National Social Work Day. Over a period of time, social work institutions have increased, but literature is very scanty on the Indianization of social work. Only a few social workers like Gandhi, Vinoba Bhave, Jyotiba Phule, etc., have given attention in Indian literature. The conferment of Bharat Ratna to Nanaji Deshmukh is a great gift to academicians, professionals and students of social work discipline in India who have been celebrating his birth anniversary on October 11 as Indian Social Work Day or Bharatiya Samaj Karya Diwas. (Dash and Shukla, 2019). However, social work scholars, thinkers, and writers have paid less attention to Nanaji Deshmukh's contribution in education, health, and rural self-reliance towards nation-building. If one neglects the contribution of Nanaji Deshmukh in the field of social work, then this omission is surprising. His sharp mind, intellect, and extraordinary skill can be acknowledged by the fact that he was noted social reformer, social activist, politician, and counted as one among the great social workers. The assessment of his legacy can be demonstrated by the practicality of Mahatma Gandhi's ideal of community development approach through self-reliance.

Nanaji's ideas and work is much similar to that of Gandhiji. Such philosophy and path breaking ideas can help, inspire and practiced by social work students and practitioners in their approach to community development. It is the time to understand his ideas and to rediscover the transcending insight of such great social worker and philosopher who gave last decades of his life in serving people at grassroots level and quitting mainstream politics.

This chapter presents Nanaji Deshmukh's thoughts as a source of social work principles, values and methods that can help in building knowledge to contemporary social work practices. Not much has been written on the contribution of Nanaji Deshmukh towards nation-building as well as community development. Surprisingly, his contribution on the subject of social work neglected and owing to this reason, the chapter has explored his work and thoughts in the field of social development, community organizing, service delivery, and conflict resolution.

It is necessary to clarify the basic concepts of approach and practice used in social work that will help to link Nanaji Deshmukh's work for community development. Social work initiative includes micro and macro level involvement of social workers (Hugman, 2009) that derive from internationally accepted social work definition. The social work profession is a helping profession that promotes social change and empowerment and freedom of people to develop or enhance well-being. In 1957, Biestek published a book *Casework Relationship* in which he successfully identified that the centrality of relationship in helping process and make it part of social work ethics. However, theories and principles of social work mediate at the point where people interrelate themselves with their environment in which they live. The principle of social justice, human rights, acceptance and non-judgmental attitude is fundamental to social work (International Association of Schools of Social Work & International Federation of Social Workers, 2004).

The word community used in this article is a self-identified social-economic residential unit or group with a self-identified set of persons with a common interest (Uphoff, 1986). Social work approach with local communities as a community development process takes place at the local level. It may be referred that such an approach encompasses community organization, social planning, advocacy, community development and ideally a social change process (Weil, 2003). It is not an ideal process that flows to the central level of planning but an enabling process that helps local people those are needy, marginalized, exploited, vulnerable and deserted from reaping benefits for their development through organizing themselves and taking responsibility for improving their social and economic condition (Midgley, 1992).

Nanaji's Idea of Community Development

The idea of community development is not new in the Indian context and almost all stalwarts of Indian polity have supported this concept. This community development practice focuses on a wide range of activities and themes and they may overlap with others. However, these community development approaches are mixed of top-down and bottom-up approaches. Although community development practice is undertaken by professional social worker or others who have inclination and interest in community development. Several known individuals have shown their passion and commitment and demonstrated effective development practice, mainly focusing on village development. For them ideal development of the country starts from the village where the maximum population resides.

Right away from Mahatma Gandhi to Rabindranath Tagore, Deen Dayal Upadhyay and Nanaji Deshmukh has always supported and dreamt about the idea of the ideal village and said that progress of India will happen only through development of village. Models like Adarsh Gram by Gandhiji, the concept of Antyodaya by Vinoba Bhave and PURA (Provision of Urban Utilities in Rural Area) by Dr. Abul Kalam Azad were few village models developed for rural community development. It is very known that Gandhian philosophy of *Sarvodaya* and other approaches are very relevant even today in the area of social work practice. But Nanaji's intervention in community development can't be ignored and side-lined because Nanaji's social work is far wider than we understand it. It is not only theoretical and philosophical but also a real-life experiment. Nanaji Deshmukh's approach was step forward to that of Mahatma Gandhi and Deen Dayal Upadhyay (Agarwal, 2020).

Nanaji's principles of community development grounded on the set of philosophical beliefs. Cooperation over competition, interdependence over self-reliance, zeal for the others over pursuit of self-interest, social justice over social injustice. The keystone of ethics of Nanaji's is service to others through which social development rests by truthfulness, acceptance, and peace for all, and helping others.

He developed a real-life community development model through his intervention for rural people. His concept of development can be looked from the angle of Gross Domestic Product (GDP) that focuses poverty alleviation by improving the economic condition of the rural people. Nanaji has emphasised on providing services that are needed by supervising, training and through consultation. Nanaji emphasises on *service*, the primary goal is to help people in need and to address social problems; *dignity and worth of person*, which emphasis "to enhance clients' capacity and opportunity to change and to address their own needs".

There may be some overlapping of concepts showing the idea of Nanaji Deshmukh's contribution to community development. This is a result of the holistic nature of Nanaji's thoughts and the way in which his real-life experiment is unfolded around social work principles, such as self-development, unity, acceptance and non-judgemental attitude.

Doctrine of Integral Humanism

Nanaji Deshmukh propagated the idea of internal humanism (Mehta, 2011). The enrichment of the foundation of integral humanism of a profession is based on basic themes of harmony, the primacy of cultural values and discipline. This approach is practically used in community development and found suitable for the holistic development of society (Sharma *et al.*, 2016, p. 5). But such moral value and theory building in social work practice has long been dominated by the belief that knowledge and theory are more critical variables in professional growth (Reamer, 1982).

His thoughts as a guide of service to human society and the pursuit of attaining social justice are complimentary to social work practice theory. His methods are based on social assistance, capacity building, self-reliance, social justice and social action, all micro and macro level. Nanaji achieved and followed this integration by neglecting ethical dilemmas in the society and accepting the doctrine of integral humanism by providing service to others irrespective of caste, race, sex, religion, etc., as approach to community development. Acceptance is considered a fundamental element of his approach by recognizing the positive work of human beings, and this principle is used as part of social work intervention (Barker, 2003). Nanaji's integral humanism doctrine rejected the model of communism and capitalism, where the value of a human is crushed and controlled by the state or elite. In contrast, Nanaji's theory supports social justice as fairness to humanity and aims at the happiness of society, giving priority to the needy and vulnerable segment of the population. The idea of social justice by Nanaji is well followed and elaborated by John Rawls (1971) in his book *'Theory of Justice.'* Rawls' principle of justice as fairness articulates the central idea that there should be equal, free and fair justice for all. Rawls gave the guiding ideas of justice as fairness in terms of equal liberties, fair equality of opportunities and the most considerable benefits to the least-advantaged population of the society. If the above condition of justice as fairness is satisfied and society is better off, than there is total equality.

Self-Reliance Campaign

Nanaji believes that despite independence, people are still slaves. Rulers and bureaucrats are enjoying the fruits of freedom. According to him, genesis of the problem relies on people's dependence on the government for anything and everything. Nanaji assumed it to be an aberration; social disintegration, unbearable economic disparity, and dreadful unemployment are seen everywhere. But, from the perspective of Nanaji, people have to take the initiative of their development.

Nanaji believes that we all are one and everyone has to live a dignified and respectful life. Dependence has increased the inequality and it has raised the laziness among the people, which is the barrier to self-reliance. The concept of self-reliance pushes us to go beyond the thinking of the world as one social system, and such practice is a part of social work education. The notion of community development creates the conditions of social and economic progress of the people only in that condition when community members come together and take active participation and fullest possible reliance upon the community development (Phillips and Pittman, 2014, p. 3) will be possible.

This theoretical concept is widely discussed, used and explored by the social workers. Nanaji's thoughts appear to have contributed in the field where he created self-sufficient model towns like Gonda and Chitrakoot. The Chitrakoot project was first self-reliance campaign launched on 26th January, 2002, at Deen Dayal Research Institute in 500 selected villages. It proves and establishes the idea of a self-reliant village community by filling the gap in government delivery system through ensuring effective implementation of government schemes. The success of the entire exercise has been adopted by the National Democratic Alliance, where they have adopted the village to make it self-reliant. Recently, the Honourable Prime Minister Narendra Modi on 7 November, 2014 under the Sansad Adarsh Gram Yojana adopted Jayapur village in the Varanasi district of Uttar Pradesh. Various corporate organizations have also adopted, such rural social work practice of adopting villages as a part of corporate social responsibility (CSR) have started growing in India.

Idea of Conflict-Free Society

Nanaji Deshmukh's idea of conflict-free society is almost the same as Mahatma Gandhi's philosophy of non-violence which is also known as *Ahimsa*. The first step to achieve the village self-resilient and prosperous is to make it free from all disputes. Conflict-free society is not just society free from dispute but conduct of positive act through mind, body and speech. Social work states that all human beings are good and kind-hearted; they all must be accepted without condition and by following the principle of non-judgemental attitude. Social work can help in resolving conflict through counselling, behaviour modification and brainstorming.

Nanaji realized that this is the first task towards rural development because a free mind is out of all encumbrances and can think of development. Conflict-free society defines the relation of one human with self and others, which forms the basis of our connections with all the life. Conflict within self—arises due to greediness towards consumerist culture. Nanaji blamed consumerism culture responsible for competition, enmity, criminal activities and litigation. Samaj Shilpi Dampattis (SSDs) is a part of Chitrakoot first self-reliance project focused on the area of the dispute-free village and help on resolving all kind of issues.

Some social work practice is done both at clinical level and community level. Clinical practice theories and techniques used to deal with client behaviour, which allows clinical social worker to intervene with the client on a one-to-one basis, whereas at community worker with the help of techniques helps in encouraging and strengthening the client or clients, i.e., individual or in a group. This concept is expanded beyond and is a part of social work practice skill where a social worker with his skill and techniques helps in conflict resolution or counselling or skill development training or advocacy etc. Social action mechanism form a promise and passion for justice. One promising development by NASW code of ethics is to recognize central importance of human relationship.

Conclusion

Nanaji once said, *"I do not stand for myself but for my kith and kin; my kith and kin are those who are oppressed and neglected"*. He was a social practitioner with practical knowledge with a high ethical standard founded in his wisdom and philosophies. Nanaji's practice was so common to that of social worker that he included concern for the empowerment of the people, social justice, self-resilience, overcoming poverty and development of the human relationship.

Nanaji's role and commitment for the betterment and development of rural development make him an exceptional role model for the social work profession. His thoughts are built on ethical ground that is followed by many scholars. Still, his thoughts have not received more considerable attention by both practitioners and academician in social work and demand for his work to be included in social work curriculum.

Knowledge building is an important part of any profession. Social work has been able to make its distinctive contribution in academic theory and practice. Nanaji's work is more than a technique for delivery of either service or justice; they are philosophical guidelines on ethical principles that help define ends and means of practice. At a time when the profession enriching its Standard Code of ethics; Principles of Social work and Community Development and encouraging the practitioners to advance social reforms more dynamically, it should systematically review Nanaji Deshmukh's thoughts and encouraging his ideas in community development process.

References

Agarwal, A. (2020). *Re-imagining Rural scape to bring changes to the lives of people in rural India.* OpIndia.https://www.opindia.com/2020/04/re-imagining-ruralscape-changes-rural-india-development-reverse-migration/ retrieved on April 17, 2020.

Barker, R. (2003). *The Social Work Dictionary* (5th ed.). Washington DC: NASW Press.

Dash, B.M. & Shukla, S. (2019). "Social Work Curriculum gets an Indian Icon", *The Pioneer*, 13 February, 2019.

Hugman, R. (2009). "But is it social Work? Some reflections on mistaken identities". *British Journal of Social Work*, 39, 1138-1153.

International Federation of Social Workers (2004). *Global standards for social work education and training.* Retrieved from http://ifsw. org/policies/global-standards/

Kumar, R. (2019). *Bharat Ratan: Nanaji Deshmukh.* India: Diamond Pocket Books.

Mehta, N. (2011). *India: A Civilization the World Fails to Recognise.* Chhattisgarh: Educreation Publishing.

Midgley, J. (1992). "Development theory, the state and social development in Asia". *Social Development Issues*, 14, 22-36.

Phillips, R., & Pittman, R. (Eds.). (2014). *An Introduction to Community Development.* Routledge.

Reamer, F. (1982). *Ethical Dilemmas in Social Service.* New York: Columbia University.

Uphoff, N. (1986). *Local Institutional Development: An Analytical Sourcebook with Cases.* West Hartford, CT: Kumarian Press.

13

Nanaji Deshmukh and his Contribution towards Nation Building

A Social Work Perspective

Sunil Prasad and *Arul Actovin C.*

Introduction

Chandikadas Amritrao Deshmukh also known as Nanaji Deshmukh was an educationist, development economist and a social activist who has worked for rural self-reliance in his entire life. His work and ideology play a vital role in influencing the social policies of the country and the social work profession. Nanaji was influenced by the ancient Indian thought and philosophy and had implemented it for the empowerment of the rural villagers. This chapter has analysed the relevance of Nanaji Deshmukh's contribution towards social work profession and its relevance for nation-building in India.

Personal Life

Nanaji Deshmukh was born in a humble family at Kadoli, in Parbhani district, Maharashtra on October 11, 1916. He had less money to pay for his tuition fees but had such a burning passion and ambition for education that he did not shy away from working as a merchant and selling vegetables to raise money to achieve his goal. Lokamanya Tilak and his nationalist views enthused him profoundly and had a keen interest in social service and related activities. His family was also in close connection with Dr. Hedgewar who was a regular visitor to Nanaji's family. He was able to discern an immense unseen potential in Nanaji and stimulated him to join the *Shakhas* of Rashtriya Swayamsevak Sangh (RSS) and his association with RSS continued for long.

Nanaji as a Politician

In 1940, following Dr. Hedgewar's death, many young people got inspired and entered in Rashtriya Swayamsevak Sangh (RSS) in Maharashtra. Nanaji was one among those inspired youths who joined the RSS and devoted his whole life in service to the country. Nanaji was sent as *Pracharak* to Uttar Pradesh and met Deendayal Upadhyaya for the first time at Agra. Nanaji went to Gorakhpur as a *Pracharak* where, through his tremendous efforts, he implemented Sangh philosophy and it was not an easy task at that time, since Sangh had no money to meet their daily expenses. He used to stay in Dharamshala while no one was allowed to stay regularly for not more than three days. Finally, Baba Raghavdas had given shelter on the condition that Nanaji would cook meals for him too. Within three years of working and around in Gorakhpur, there were two hundred and five Sangh Shakhs. It has been his hard work. Nanaji always had given great importance on education and founded India's first Saraswati Sishu Mandir at Gorakhpur in 1950 which represents Nanaji's love for education and knowledge.

In 1947, RSS launched two journals namely "Rashtradharma" and "Panchjanya" and a newspaper called "Swadesh". In these publications where Atal Bihari Vajpayee worked as the editor and Deendayal Upadhyaya was made the Margdarshak with Nanaji as the Managing Director. It was a challenging task as the organization had to publish these publications despite financial constraints. However, due to such financial difficulties he never lost the spirit and these publications gained acceptance and popularity among common people. Rashtriya Swayam Sevak Sangh was banned due to Mahatma Gandhi's assassination and it led to difficulty to publish journals and newspaper of RSS. Nanaji used a different strategy for underground publication work by the RSS those days.

Janata Party Movement

Nanaji was inspired by Vinoba Bhave and joined the Bhoodan movement energetically, and movement was successful. Nanaji had given his full support to Jaiprakash Narayan for the movement which he called "Total Revolution". Nanaji played vital role for formation of Janata Party and he was one of its main architects. Nanaji was elected as Member of Parliament from Balrampur constituency of the state of Uttar Pradesh and was not willing join in Morarji Desai's ministry. He politely refused it. Nanaji considered politics as mission but not as career that's the reason he announced his stepping down from politics at the age of sixty. He was the only politician who willingly announced his retirement from politics. Later, he became a permanent social worker in his remaining life.

Foray into Electoral Politics

Nanaji Deshmukh was a founding member of the Jan Sangh and a long-time RSS member. He considered politics as a mission never a career. He never looked back to politics after he announced retirement of his own decision. He started working as a social worker soon after he quit public life. In one of his interviews, when *India Today* magazine interviewed him about his unexpected choice to quit politics, he said "It is an ultiduniya (upside down world) that we are creating. India's wealth, both in terms of people and natural resources, is in her villages. But the Government is ignoring that. It is developing only cities and promoting consumerism. Disgusted with politicians, I decided to use young people to see what could be done in villages." Nanaji also stated, "There is no Hindu-Muslim problem in our country and is all created by politicians. That is one of the reasons I quit politics" for his views on the Hindu-Muslim relations (Bhaumik, 1997).

Rural Development

In 1969, Nanaji Deshmukh established Deendayal Research Institute (DRI) which is a non-governmental organisation dedicated for strengthening various developmental activities to nation. Since the establishment of the institute, it has been functioning for the improvement of the underprivileged, marginalised and poor people including tribals in central India (B.L. Manjunatha, 2017). The first university which dedicated to rural development "Chitrakoot Gramodaya Vishwavidyalay" was established by Nanaji in Chitrakoot on February 12, 1991. This university was based upon the philosophy of Mahatma Gandhi and Deendayal Upadhyaya as well as learnings and experiences of his social work models were based upon above mentioned two great personalities. He also served as first Chancellor of the university (B.L. Manjunatha, 2017).

Samaj Shilpi Dampati (SSD)

In 1996, the Deendayal Research Institute developed an innovative concept of grassroots level functionaries to reaching development works in village known as *Samaj Shilpi Dampati* (SSD) and its literally meaning is society sculptor couple. SSD is a model in which a newly married graduate couple with the sense of commitment towards community service for the villages and these couples were staying in villages (a cluster of five villages) for a period of five years and was engaged in the implementation of various community development activities in the remote tribal areas. In Bundelkhand region, nine SSD couples joined under this scheme to work (B.L. Manjunatha, 2017). Deendayal Research Institute's village developmental model is a unique way of implementing various developmental activities were most suited for the country. Deendayal Research Institute believed that people's power is stronger than political power (Kalam, 2005a; Kalam, 2005b; Kalam, 2005c).

The Chitrakoot Project

In 2002, Deendayal Research Institute (DRI) had launched a Chitrakoot Project. The Chitrakoot Project was developed based upon the principles of Deendayal Upadhyaya's theory of integral humanism to promote inclusive model for the development of rural India. This project was planned and was based upon a model which covers to address the problems of agriculture, income, education, health, hygiene, social conscience and conservation of resource (DRI, 2002). The Chitrakoot project has applied "Participatory Rural Appraisal" technique that emphasises on a bottom up approach for improvement in five hundred villages around the Chitrakoot area covering two states namely, Uttar Pradesh and Madhya Pradesh. Nanaji believed that the villagers' participation is very much important for development of the community as well as to fulfil the needs of a specific village people. Through the participation of the villagers and based upon their suggestions, various development programmes were initiated and implemented under this project in villages (Deendayal Research Institute, 2016).

Nanaji as a Social Worker

Though Nanaji's developmental activities were evolved through Mahatma Gandhi's ideology where Gandhi had viewed rural development will be possible through the implementation of various development activities in villages with bottom up approach as well as to identify and to develop dedicated social workers who lived within the community itself which will lead to sustained interaction with the villagers to realise their difficulties and encourage them to change (Gandhi, 1927), Gandhi's philosophy of rural development was based on the principles of people-centred values (humanism, justice, faith in people), non-violence, development orientation and value base for social work (Gandhi, 1962; Desai and Narayan, 1998; Narayan, 2000). Both Tagore and Nanaji viewed rural reconstruction starts with educational development as foundation and observed "reform of education and generation of villages are the major tasks of my life" (Tagore, 1972). So, Nanaji has emphasized on quality education for the children.

The role of social work is enshrined in a collection of basic values, and those values are dignity and worth of the person, service and importance of human relationships, social justice, integrity and competence which are incorporated by social workers during the profession's history. Besides that social workers must emphasise the Indic values of social work, *dharma*, *satya*, *ahimsha*, *nishtha*.

(Dash, *et al.*, 2019). "Social workers are responsible for self-reflecting on the impact on their professional and personal life of their own cultural beliefs" (NASW, 2001). The professional social worker envisions a society which is free from any types of conflicts, without any discrimination where equality prevails, poverty is eradicated, and where full of opportunities are there. Social worker's concern for socially deprived people, ideal of intimate family ties, concept of nutrition and health care for everyone, fight for social justice, decentralization of power and efforts to reduce the gap between poor and rich (Kumar, 1995).

Nanaji also understood that development must be done from the viewpoint of disadvantaged people and started various community developmental activities to ensure self-reliance, development of health and education in the areas of Chitrakoot. Nanaji's contribution to social service had been recognised and he was nominated to the Rajya Sabha in 1999 for his services to the nation. On 27th February, 2010, Nanaji died in Chitrakoot and later in 2019, he was awarded India's highest civilian's award Bharat Ratna.

Both Nanaji's thought and Social Work profession express the go forward to social change which is progressive and for the improvement of any society. From professional social work perspectives, Nanaji's rural community developmental activities through Deendayal Research Institute had significant role in community organization method as well as this programme mostly focused on development of the villages as well as individuals. Moreover all of his actions are closely connected with community advocacy which is reflected as one of the significant methods of professional social work. Indeed he has developed the most appropriate method of social work consistent with Indian culture and conditions. Nanaji's approach was similar to that of the professional social worker indeed he prepared the ground for the strengthening of the social work profession in India. Hence, Nanaji and Social Work profession have a connection which aims at common goals and objectives which can be achieved through different approaches to a current scenario. Nanaji worked through various developmental activities for rural community development which fits skilfully with social work theory.

Conclusion

As a person Nanaji had a tough exterior, but he was very soft by heart. Nothing was personal for him. He was just like an open book. Really Nanaji was a real 'Nana'. Dr. A.P.J. Abdul Kalam admired him for his "single-minded devotion to the uplift of the people". Nanaji's concerns about the future of India were all reverberated in his various community development activities and they remain for us as a guide in our future actions. The professional social worker can enrich themselves from Nanaji ideology and thought as it is a depot of extensive knowledge based on ground realities and issues and ethical concepts which would help the social worker to define the ends and means of any practice. Even in today's context, Nanaji's idea can solve community issues in the Indian society. Undoubtedly, Nanaji's appeal was very emotional but it was not based merely on emotions and he lived as a committed social worker who lives within the community for its development. Nanaji Deshmukh promoted social harmony as he believes that it is the ultimate goal of every social worker in his/her life.

References

Bakshi, S.R. (1986). *Gandhi and his social thought*. Criterion Publications, New Delhi.

Bhaumik, S.N. (1997, August 11). *India Today Magazine*. Retrieved June 12, 2020, from India Today: https://www.indiatoday.in/magazine/profile/story/19970811-hindu-muslim-problem-a-creation-of-politicians-nanaji-deshmukh-8318811-997081#ssologin=1#source= magaine

Desai, M. and Narayan, L. (1998). "Challenges for social work profession towards people-centred development", In Desai, M. Monteiro, A. and Narayan, L. (Eds.) *Towards People-Centred Development*, Part 2, pp. 531-58, Tata Institute of Social Sciences, Mumbai.

DRI. (2002). Sustainable watershed management for national prosperity, Deendayal Research Institute and District Rural Development Agency, Satna, Madhya Pradesh, June 2002, p. 6.

Deendayal Research Institute. (2016). *Deendayal Research Institute*. Retrieved June 10, 2020, from Chitrakoot: http://www.chitrakoot.org/html/index.htm

Dash, B.M., Ramesh, B., Parshurama, K.G., and Kumar, M. (2019). *New Frontiers in Social Work Practice: Bharatiya Contexts, Perspectives and Experiences*, Tumkur University, Karnataka, pp. 1-9.

Gandhi, M.K. (1927). *The Story of My Experiments with Truth*, Ahmedabad: Navjivan Publishing House.

Gandhi, M.K. (1962). *True Education*, Ahmedabad: Navjivan Publishing House.

Kalam, A. (2005a). President's speech in Patni, DRI Chitrakoot, 6 October, 2005.

Kalam, A. (2005b). President's address at the 52nd National Film Awards Ceremony, Vigyan Bhawan, New Delhi on October 21, 2005.

Kalam, A. (2005c). President's address at the National conference of Legal empowerment on the occasion of National Legal Literacy Day, Vigyan Bhavan, New Delhi on November 11, 2005.

Kumar, H. (1995). *Theories in Social Work Practice*. New Delhi: Friends Publications (India).

Narayan, L. (2000). "Freire and Gandhi: Their relevance for social work education." *Intl. Social Work*, 43 (2): 193-204.

National Association of Social Workers (2001). NASW standards for cultural competence in social work practice. National Association of Social Workers.

Tagore, R. (1972). *Siksha*. Visva-Bharati Granthan Vibhaga, Calcutta, p. 20.

14
Sustainable Development Through Law
A Real Tribute to Bharat Ratna, Nanaji Deshmukh

J.K.L. Sujatha

Introduction

Sustainable Development is a balance between Environment and Development. Right to Environment and Right to Development are integral part of Right to life and personal liberty under Article 21 of the Indian Constitution.[1] Despite various developmental programmes, the basic problems of inclusive growth, the security of food, Primary Education and Primary health to each and every Indian still remains a dream and a majority of the people are still living below poverty line.

The United Nations Conference on Sustainable Development (UNCSD), which witnessed the gathering of UN member-states and other stakeholders in Brazil in 2012, is a key occasion to take stock of 20 years of action at all levels to promote sustainable development, and to provide a clear vision and way forward for the international community, national governments, partnerships and other stakeholders in implementing the sustainable development agenda in an integrated manner.

Knowledge must inform action-knowledge of what has and has not worked for sustainable development in the past 20 years, knowledge as well of important changes and new challenges that have emerged in the past generation needs to be looked into. Only on this basis can we develop a clear vision of sustainable development for the 21st century. That vision needs to incorporate and built upon the rich output of various global assessments, including climate change, water, energy, and ecosystems—as well as the policy lessons from experience, respond to the evolving nature of the challenges, and draw upon the latest research on integrating sustainability and development into a common agenda. It also needs to recognize and motivate the contribution of all inhabitants of planet earth.

Over the last years rural activity or farming has faced several hurdles in regard to development and evolution. Generational transfer is one of the problems, though not the only one or the most serious. There are still grave disparities all-over the world between urban and country life.

Rural development is about a process that seeks social change and sustainable economic development for the rural community's ongoing progress. The ultimate goal is to improve their quality of life and preserve the environment.

There are three basic needs in rural development for a sustainable future:

1. Improving the lives of the millions of the people in the country (nearly half of the world population), thus reducing the rural-urban gap, stamping out poverty and preventing city migration.
2. Protecting and preserving natural landscape and cultural resources.
3. Ensuring universal access to food with a sustainable farming production.

The 2013 World Monitoring Report of the Millennium Development Goals (MDGs) confirmed that the rural-urban gap still existed in the whole world. Illiteracy, lack of health care or poverty is some of the common problems affecting the country. Bharat Ratna Nanaji Deshmukh's social work model of integral humanism based upon Indian Knowledge Systems for achieving Sustainable Development Goals which is the need of the hour. The constitutional framework, Fundamental Rights, Directive Principles of State Policy and Fundamental Duties, the Dignity of Individual Goals of the Society aiming Equality, Freedom, Decent Life with Human Dignity, and Socialistic Pattern of Society through democratic decentralization aims at welfare of the human beings.

Village panchayat, inclusive growth, Sustainable Development, Integral Humanism are envisaged and sincere attempts were made to achieve and realize these Constitutional Values. Nanaji Deshkmukh's social work models are effective tools to achieve Gram Swaraj and self-sufficiency of villages based upon Ancient Indian Knowledge Systems based upon freedom-oriented people's participation in the development process. The Constitution of India provides the base to work upon different viable efficient models. An attempt is made in this chapter to understand the Sustainable Development Goals, in the backdrop of Chitrakoot Model of Nanaji Deshmukh for sustainable village development and need and necessity of application of Nanaji Deshmukh model throughout India. Nanaji placed people at the centre of development and wanted the society to take the lead. He believed in collective responsibility and collective efforts to transform rural areas into thriving hubs of economic activities. In a way, he was the pioneer of the present day corporate social responsibility and had in those days inspired many industrialists to contribute towards social causes.

Present government's Swachh Bharat programme is an example of people's participation in transforming the nation. Swachh Bharat has now become a people's movement and is contributing hugely in changing the mindset of the masses – from celebrities to common man. Deendayal Research Institute (DRI), set-up on March 8, 1968 under the inspirational guidance of Padam Vibhushan Shri Nanaji Deshmukh is currently working to validate the philosophy of "Integral Humanism". Models for development such as providing services for health, hygiene, basic education, training for self-employment etc. have been developed to achieve overall socio-economic development and reconstruction of Indian Society. The developmental programmes have been carried out at various centres viz. Delhi, Gonda, Balrampur (U.P.), Chitrakoot (U.P. & M.P.), Beed, Nagpur (Maharashtra).

The mission statement of Deendayal Research Institute is **'We are not for ourselves but for our kith and kin. Our kith and kins are those who are oppressed and neglected'**. The aim of the Institute is to evolve a social system for the transformation of our age old Indian society suited to the modern scientific era and based on eternal values of integral Humanism. With this aim Deendayal Research Institute has undertaken following major programmes:

- To carry out research in Social Science with a view to reconstruct Indian society.
- To establish Rural Development and Training centres for carrying out research with a view to motivate people in adopting new and improved technologies in the field of sustainable Agriculture, Water Conservation and Alternative Industrialization and promote self-employment.
- Activities in the field of medical research, medical care, life-long health and medical education.
- To set-up Academic and Technical Vocational Training centres in rural areas.
- To eradicate social evils by propagating human values with the active cooperation and initiative of the people.
- To establish Dispute free Society.
- Integrated Tribal Development.
- To ensure people's initiative and active participation in the efforts.
- To organize Intellectual Activities.
- To share the experience and Intellectual property with other Organizations.

Our Constitution envisages India as a Sovereign, Socialist, Secular, Democratic Republic imbibing the aims and aspirations of the people of India and these have been translated into the various provisions of the Constitution. All governmental organs and institutions owe their origin to the Constitution and derive their powers from their provisions. These organs and institutions enjoy only such powers as are conferred on them and function within limits demarcated by the Constitution. Judiciary is no exception. Parliament is accountable to the people directly. The executive is accountable to the Parliament. Judiciary is accountable to the Constitution itself.

The Constitution aims at the creation of new legal norms, social philosophy and economic values which are to be reflected by striking synthesis, harmony and fundamental adjustment between individual rights and social interests to achieve the desired community goals. Constitutional morality would mean effective coordination between conflicting interests of different people and the administrative cooperation to resolve them amicably without any confrontation amongst the various groups working for the realization of their ends at any cost.

Theoretical Foundations of Individual and Social Rights

The conflict between individual rights and claims of the society is an inevitable struggle in any progressive society. The liberal conception of rights differs significantly from the tradition, which views rights as naturally inherent in the Human Person. By contrast, liberals start by devising a general political theory from which they then seek to derive a series of rights. H.L.A. Hart also commented rights-based theories have replaced utilitarianism.

Kant favours maximum equal liberty to each individual. The law of nature was considered by Kant as a principle of human reason. According to him, the law of reason was not influenced by external factors. Law of the reason is a moral imperative. It is categorical, obligatory in the form of command directing the human will do what is morally good for all times and place irrespective of ends, considerations or selfish devices. Natural law was again revived based on moral idealism in the 20th century. The revival of natural law promoted the idea that certain moral and ethical ideals of Justice are necessarily related to law and its content.

The formation of U.N.O. and Universal Declaration of Human Rights and the two covenants on political and civil rights and economic and social rights are the results of the recognition of the importance of Natural Law and Natural Rights in the 20th century. At the national level, various Constitutions guaranteed the basic human rights in the form of Bill of Rights, Fundamental Rights and Directive Principles of State Policy. Thus, this Kantian theory has a tremendous influence in the twentieth century which also had its impact on the great philosopher John Rawls.

Human Capabilities for Effective Enforcement of Human Rights

Utilitarianism and Political Liberalism are two major philosophical trends in contemporary political philosophy. Utilitarianism maximizes the happiness of the greatest number of people in society with minimum friction. Developmental activities such as constructing huge dams, establishing huge power plants, promoting privatization and economic liberalization are supported by Utilitarianism Amartya Sen's Human Capabilities and Freedom as the measure of human development further developed by Martha C. Nussbaum into capabilities approach. According to Nussbaum, women, children, elderly and disabled people were excluded by Social contract theories. Social contract tradition states sovereign equality. But a powerful global economy makes all economic choices. Even the last work the *Laws of People* (1999) of Rawls proves inadequate to solve the problem of justice among nationals as it ignores the impact of economic globalization. The question of justice involving non-human animals is not addressed by social contract tradition as social contract makes among rational human society.

The work of Nussbaum is a constructive critique of Rawls Theory of Justice. Her alternative is the capabilities approach to social justice. The capabilities are presented as the source of political principles for a liberal pluralist society. The capability approach sides with Indian Constitution which is influenced by the Ambedkar Social Philosophy and against the neoliberal interpretation of the U.S. Constitution. It makes clear that securing a right to someone requires more than the absence of negative state action. Nussbaum's capabilities approach has great relevance for the current Indian debate on the issues of Social Empowerment in the context of Economic Globalization and its impact on the marginalized and disadvantaged people and the debate about socially inclusive growth. Recently, Amartya Sen in 'Idea of Justice' argued removal of inequality is justice.[2]

Making Human Rights a Reality—A Real Tribute to Bharat Ratna Nanaji Deshmukh's Social Work Model of Integral Humanism

Article 28 of the Universal Declaration of Human Rights provides:

'Everyone is entitled to a social and international order in which the rights and freedoms set forth in the Declaration can be fully realized.' Can we state that the present 'international order' guarantees the implementation of all human rights? Can it assure the realization of legitimate aspirations of humankind to international and internal peace, to human rights, to sustainable development, to democratization? Is the elaboration of an effective common policy to meet scientific, technological and environmental challenges possible?

More than half a century ago, the President of the United States, Franklin D. Roosevelt, while thinking about a new world order to be established after the end of the Second World War, proposed to base it on four freedoms: the freedom of speech and expression, the freedom of every person to worship God in his own way, the freedom from want and the freedom from fear. None of these four freedoms can be recognized as being already guaranteed in the existing international order. To achieve this goal, the international system should have the possibility of dealing with the main obstacles and threats to human rights, such as extreme poverty, exclusion, underdevelopment, discrimination, intolerance or terrorism. The international community should have the ability to address the real causes of conflicts. It demands further structural adjustments in the United Nations system. Though the creation of the post of the United Nations High Commissioner for Human Rights may be seen as the first step in this direction, there is perhaps a need for the establishment of a new principal organ or body with much stronger competencies and responsibilities. However, such a new role and further involvement of the United Nations in the protection of human rights are determined by the political will of Member States, their readiness to accept new legal, economic and social measures.[3]

The progress of democratization in many parts of the world poses new questions concerning democratization of the international system advancement of democracy, though in many countries of rather 'low density', is to a great degree a function of the development of civil societies: participation of individuals and groups in decision-making processes, in the democratic governance of their countries. What is the place of a global society in international relations?

How should non-governmental organizations, which undeniably become a spirituous mover of progress in the field of human rights, be represented in international structures and organs? Should individuals and groups become subjects of international law? What are the international consequences of the recognition of rights and responsibilities of individuals, groups and organs of society to promote and protect universally recognized human rights and fundamental freedoms? National institutions, non-governmental organizations, academic institutions and grassroots initiatives should be fully accepted as natural human rights advocates and partners in international human rights cooperation.

The construction of an international order in which all human rights and freedoms, including economic, social and cultural as well as the right to development, can be fully realized, in which all human rights could be guaranteed for all, has become the most important human rights challenge for the twenty-first century. The task has theoretical implications, though it is evident that progress is needed in the use of existing instruments and in the building of new legal frameworks. There must be above all considerable and decisive progress in our understanding of the forms of social interdependence. For that, we need first of all to learn all the lessons from the 'objection' of the poor. This is not new; human rights have always advanced in this way, by learning from victims. "Unfortunately, people rapidly forget what they owe in this way to the poorest of the poor from age to age. Today they appear in particular to have forgotten that they owe to them a conception of man as born equal, free and essential to the lives of others."

Any social work model should reflect the basic human rights approach. Nanaji Deshmukh's integral humanism is totally based upon the above natural rights, philosophy which is the backbone for human rights jurisprudence in India or elsewhere. Today, even after 70 years of Independence, the country is facing various challenges like poverty, illiteracy, lack of skills among youth and urban-rural divide to name a few. Collective efforts are needed to overcome these challenges and people should be in the forefront of complementing the initiatives of the government. In fact, the constitution lists several fundamental duties of the citizens and one of them is "to strive towards excellence in all spheres of individual and collective activity so that the nation constantly rises to higher levels of endeavour and achievements." For deepening the roots of democracy and strengthening pluralism, it is important for people across the social strata to contribute in a conscientious manner towards building an egalitarian, healthy, inclusive and responsive society. Progress can be achieved only when there is peace, social, communal and cultural harmony.[4]

Hon'ble Prime Minister has highest regards towards "Nanaji Deshmukh's stellar contribution towards rural development as he showed the way for a new paradigm of empowering those living in our villages. He personifies humility, compassion, and service to the downtrodden. He is a Bharat Ratna in the truest sense. The Rural Development is possible when Nanaji Deshmukh's social work model of integral humanism is applied in practice settings. It is really noteworthy to appreciate the present central government for Swachh Bharat and other community development programmes. The relevance of Nanaji Deshmukh's integral humanism today is highly felt by the Indian society.

Notes

1. *Sustainable Urban and Rural Development:* A section of *Sustainability.*
2. Amartya Sen (2009), *'Idea of Justice'*, New Delhi: Sage Publications.
3. By treating law of reason as moral imperative, i.e. categorical imperative, Emmanuel Kant secularized the natural thinking. Neo-Kantians like Stamler developed this concept further.
4. Address by Shri M. Venkaiah Naidu, Honourable Vice President of India at the 8th Nanaji Memorial Lecture organized by the Deendayal Research Institute, in New Delhi on June 1, 2018.

15

Chasing Swachh Bharat Abhiyan Through Nana Deshmukh Way

The Visionary Social Worker

Chandrakala Diyali

Introduction

'Swachhata' has always been the way of life for Indians, which was strongly emphasized by even our Father of the Nation. The same concept has recently been reiterated into a gigantic nationwide movement when our Prime Minister Shri Narendra Modi held the broom to formally launch the Swachh Bharat Mission at Rajpath in New Delhi, on 2nd October 2014, to realize the dream of 'Clean India' under the aegis of 'UN Sustainable Development Goals' of 2015. The Government and other stakeholders have been striving hard to realize this goal, but it is now already high time, the Government zeroed its focus on the most alarming concern that is pollution through the polythene and plastic materials for it being 'Non-Biodegradable' in nature, than any other biodegradable materials (which would ultimately melt in the soil through a natural process) in more effective manner. The repercussions of overdependency has led to over-production without having proper mechanism to recycle, which are being unmindfully disposed in the environment that has placed humans and all organism (land, air and water) in an irreversible danger and has pushed diverse and exotic species to the brink of extinction. Hence, by the way of this study, the author would like to use the Content Analysis methodology to present the viewpoint through the lenses of our father of the Social Work, Shri Nanaji Deshmukh had incorporated the solution finding appropriate or cost-effective alternatives to make the movement successful in the way he has shown the path of 'People's participation through mass awakening' at the grassroots and localised level, to mobilise them to be equal partner in delivering its duties to collect the existing non-biodegradable materials and advocate for its complete ban of its use in all areas, realizing the goal of making India come to the Global Map in terms of its 'cleanliness'.

The harmonious co-existence between man and nature is a part of our natural heritage that gets manifested in our culture and traditional practices and in our lifestyles, that calls our planet Mother Earth. The environmental sustainability, which focuses on both Intra-generational and Inter-generational equity, has been the approach of Indians since the historical times. Modern life that has driven the mankind with individualistic aspiration and greed over community living and its welfare has already started showing very ugly repercussion on the environment. The concept of development itself has lost the track in the face of unprecedented mass production of manufactured goods, optimum profit, irrational consumerism concrete jungle that merely has a bull eye focus on amassing the wealth that has led to irreparable and permanent destruction and damage to our diverse and exotic flora and fauna disrupting the sustainability of life on Mother Earth.

Plastics are symptomatic of this most unsustainable, blind and greed-oriented development. Due to plastic's versatility, light weight and relatively cheaper cost of production. The use of single use plastic items has become indispensable part of our daily life. The unmanaged plastic waste has not only become a challenge for cities and rural areas alike but also for our oceans and rivers across the globe as it is contaminating our soil, air and water. "Plastics are non-biodegradable; they do not vanish from the face of the Earth that may take more than 500 years for a plastic bag in a landfill to completely break down or never." After these plastic comes under the influence of extreme weather condition it triggers chemical reactions in the materials molecular structure which break it down, further posing a new problem—micro-plastics that gets carried through our food chain.

Plastic was recognized as a multifaceted material and experienced widespread usage starting from the 1950s. Since then, it has transcended the boundaries of space and time to become universal in nature, and has established a global footprint, being found even in the most remote locations. It is estimated that the production of plastics has increased exponentially from 2.3 million tons in 1950 to 335 million tons in 2016 and is expected to triple by 2050 while consuming 20 per cent of the global annual crude oil. The productions of plastic products are not managed for recycling that is only designed for single use.

According to recent data, the 40 per cent of plastics produced across the world is for packaging, which is single-use and is thrown away. In the Asian market alone, 500 million tons of plastic was produced across all industries in 2015. 448 million tons was produced across multiple sectors including building and construction, industrial machinery, transportation, electrical, textiles, consumer products, and packaging—and another 52 million tons was produced in the healthcare and agricultural sectors. As of 2017, a report by the Central Pollution Control Board which studied data from 60 major cities across India concluded that 25,940 tons of plastic is being generated per day. An alarming 43 per cent of that total is used in packaging and single use plastic. What can be understood from these statistics is that India's hyper-consumeristic nature has not only caught up with, but grossly outpaced this country's ability to recycle.

Excess plastic littered along roads and water bodies, coupled with industries dumping their waste into rivers results in currents carrying this material downstream. This becomes a venomous pyroclastic flow of sludge like material, constituted of plastics and toxic waste—eventually spewing into our oceans to form vortexes of debris which amount to 80,000 tons of slurry waste as is seen in the Great Pacific Garbage Patch. Plastic waste chokes the drainage networks of urban and rural settlements alike—resulting in sewers overflowing and water stagnating in pestilent pools which become centres for vectors like mosquitoes as they carry viral diseases to humans and animals. In Delhi, plastic finds its way onto limited precious patches of greenery where it deteriorates soil quality and leeches its harmful toxins into the ground. It is "consumed by livestock [and] also finds its way into the food chain."

Review of Literature

Prime Minister Narendra Modi in a tweet on Friday (January 25, 2019), responded to the announcement of Bharat Ratna being conferred upon Deshmukh, mentioned that 'Nanaji Deshmukh's stellar contribution towards rural development showed the way for a new paradigm of empowering those living in our villages. He personifies humility, compassion and service to the downtrodden. He is a Bharat Ratna in the truest sense'.

According to Abraham Flexner (1915), Social Work is not a single model such as that of health, followed by medical professions such as nurses and doctors, but an integrated profession, and the likeness with media profession is that social work requires a continued study for professional development to retain knowledge and skills that are evidence-based by practice standards.

Shri Mukul Kanitkar, the eminent author and social thinker said Bharat Ratna Nanaji Deshmukh institutionalized the Bharatiya concept of social service into professional social work. Prof. Rajneesh Kumar Shukla, Vice-Chancellor, MGAHV, said, the primary objective of Nanaji's social work was development that was to create dedicated persons for society. Norwegian diplomat and previous Head of UN Environment, Erik Solheim Giacovelli, Claudia in the report *Single Use Plastics: A Roadmap for Sustainability*, United Nations Environment Programme, 2018 stated that Plastic being described as a 'miracle material' by its ubiquitous nature as a cheap material has enabled unprecedented advances in "the health sector, the growth of clean energy from wind turbines and solar panel and safe food storage." However, because of its ubiquity, and the materials multipurpose nature, it has come to pose one of the greatest environmental challenges to the world today.

The United Nations Environment Programme has recognized its significant contributions to society and the benefits it has provided through a SWOT analysis. Listed below are some of the advantages of conventional plastic materials:

A SWOT analysis is used in identifying a subject matter's strengths, weaknesses, opportunities, and threats.

Kershaw, Peter in the report exploring the potential for adopting alternative materials to reduce marine plastic litter, United Nations Environment Programme, May 2018, "Improved human health outcomes from medical applications, packaging reduces food wastage from field to market and market to consumer, lower water and energy consumption in production, lower fuel consumption in aviation and vehicular transport, packaging reduces damage to goods during transport, [and] convenience to consumers, including 'take away' or 'fast-food' applications." Research done by the scientific community shows that "it's unclear how long it will take for plastic to completely biodegrade into its constituent molecules. Estimates range from 450 years to never" (*Ibid.,* Parker).

India provides a new set of harsh climatic conditions which batter plastic waste strewn about, with severe 45 degree summer heat waves and torrential downpours. These aggressive weather conditions trigger chemical reactions in the materials molecular structure which break it down, further posing a new problem—micro-plastics. Plastic as an element never completely degrades, but further breaks down into smaller micro-fragments of over a long period of time. These tiny particles leech their toxins into soil, and combine with water—eventually posing an even greater threat to humans and animals—bio magnification. Bio magnification is "the process by which a compound (such as a pollutant or pesticide) increases its concentration in the tissues of organisms as it travels up the food chain." (*Bio magnification*, Merriam-Webster.com. 2009)

"Persistent bio-accumulative and toxic (PBTs) chemicals or substances pose a risk to the marine environment because they resist degradation, persisting for years or even decades. PBTs are toxic to humans and marine organisms and have been shown to accumulate at various trophic levels through the food chain. Even at low concentrations, PBTs can be insidious in the environment due to their ability to bio magnify up the food web, leading to toxic effects at higher trophic levels." (Toxicological Threats of Plastic, United States Environmental Protection Agency).

According to the report of Anatomy of the Endocrine System, Johns Hopkins Medical, Prolonged consumption of these toxic chemicals is known to be fatal to the health of all organisms—having the ability to disrupt the endocrine system. The endocrine system is comprised of a network of glands which exudes hormones "to control and coordinate your body's metabolism, energy level, reproduction, growth and development, and response to injury, stress, and mood."

Bharat Ratna Chandikadas Amritrao Deshmukh-Nanaji Deshmukh's Contribution in Sustainable Development

It is a long awaited journey to Indianise the Profession of Social Work and designate the Title of Father of the Indian Social Work to our Bharat Ratna Chandikadas Amritrao Deshmukh (11th October, 1916 to 27th February, 2010), popularly known as Nanaji Deshmukh who perceived needs of his people during his time brought in the inner awakening of the people through awareness generation and emphasise on the concept of community participation for the sustainable development of individual, society and country that was shown in the Chitrakoot experiment of Gramodaya (village development) which included a structured training programme for the activists grooming them into professional social workers.

He advocated for self-reliance of every locality, for laying the foundation of sustainable development. He carried his strategy of development on the framework of the ancient Indian knowledge and presented an integrated model of sustainable development in every sector like economy, socio-cultural, political and last but not the least, environment/ecology and other related sectors. His contribution as an epitome of Social Work is so distinctive as when the world is now trying hard to race towards the sustainable development with our International body UN declaring SDGs in 2015 to achieve by members by 2030. He conceived the need for sustainability through self-reliance much ahead of his time in different setting and areas. He started the systematic, scientific and more organized social work by applying the principles of service or *Sewa* in professional manner laying the strong foundation of tradition of Indian Social Work. The Chitrakoot Gramoday University, Madhya Pradesh and over 450 villages where he worked are eye witnesses to his contributions in social work from Indian perspective.

Unlike Western idea of Individualistic society and service, our country is known for community living and its welfare and development of one and all hence Nanaji was a real guide towards implementing sustainable integral humanism in the field of social work. His social work models, field-work and practices all have imprints of integral humanism.

The Indian Social Work that Nanaji focused was Integrated or Holistic Development by following the path of Sustainable Development for not only human population but all the living organisms, flora and fauna and other physical elements on this planet therefore now when we are at the threshold of facing a catastrophe due to hyper development based on 'Minting Maximum profits' and 'insane consumerism' ignoring the ethics and values of sustainable development that has led to relentless production and use of Non-Biodegradable plastics that is very toxic and leading to silent extinction of our diverse flora and fauna endangering the very survival of human species in near future as it has already entered the water and food cycle/chain.

Learnings from Nanaji's Dedicated Work on Sustainable Development

The following are the solution the author can put forth to combat the menace of plastic pollution in all element of our earth:

- Mass awakening to combat the plastic pollution through mass participation.
- Use the Programme Media or Mass Media to make people aware about harmfulness of plastic to one and all on the earth.
- Generating self-consciousness among civil society to avoid the use of plastics.
- Advocate through procession, banner and propaganda to ban the source-manufacturing, sale and its use.
- Voice for social change through legislation to completely ban the manufacturing, production, sale and its use at the grassroots and localised level.

- To mobilise the Civil Society to be equal partner in delivering its duties to collect the existing non-biodegradable materials and advocate for its complete ban of its use in all areas.
- Mass participation to incorporate the solution finding appropriate or cost-effective alternatives to make the movement successful in the way Nanaji has shown the path of self-reliance.
- To avail alternative materials such as natural or plant-based polymers provide a possible solution for this growing problem. Plant-based polymers are organic in nature and are biodegradable. It "utilizes renewable natural resources, potential to be carbon neutral, provides social and economic opportunities in rural areas for vulnerable groups in society, can be composted in a domestic or industrial facility or decomposed by anaerobic digestion, biodegradable in the environment.
- Another approach is finding responsible ways to dispose of and recycle plastic through community mobilization and sensitization efforts. *Sarthak Samudayik Vikas Evam Jan Kalyan Sanstha* (Sarthak) is one such organization that is working on these issues.
- Empowering community—the city's trash collectors. Collectivizing and institutionalizing them into a Self Help Group—a mobilized and self-sustainable unit of individuals to bring about significant social change.
- The Municipal Corporation collect and segregate tons of waste per day hence NGOs and other Civil Societies can establish a public-private partnership with the support of Environment and Housing Department is another way to curtail and completely ban the plastics use.
- The Corporate Social Responsibilities should also focus on sustainable development and work towards banning the non-biodegradable products.
- The International body and other stakeholders should carry on the movement of combatting Non-Biodegradable materials in a holistic manner and start focusing on sustainable alternative use.

Conclusion

The author strongly believes that the messages and facts presented in this chapter will compel every individual to contribute in saving the environment by following the principle of refuse, reduce, reuse, recycle of the existing Non-Biodegradable Plastics and even advocate for its complete ban from source to the use, as rightly being taught by our Social Work icon Sri Nanaji Deshmukhji as how each person's dedicated work in the society can bring in positive result of welfare of all the creatures on earth. At the same time, we must join hands to tackle this challenge at the local level with the ultimate aim of making the movement at global level as has been guided by the objective of Nanaji Deshmukh's social work from Gonda to Chitrakoot to create dedicated persons for society. This is because if such persons are created, the social work will be based on and supported by the society which would lead to the liberation of the entire society from all the evils to reach the goal of self-reliance.

Plastic waste is crossing national borders through our waterways and oceans. These trans-boundary challenges need global efforts therefore we must channelize every stakeholder to work for society with one's own individual goodwill and noble intentions as advocated by our Father of Social Work. From a solid waste management challenges to the plastic menace highlighting the key messages for individuals and organizations on how to deal with plastics in a holistic manner. The essence of sustainability being taught by Nanaji Deshmukh has shown us the path of selfless service to society and in a holistic manner. So the creation of a self-reliant society is an ideal to be achieved through unselfish social service.

Hence, not only the Professional Social Workers the world at large should work with dedication and with full deep-seated commitment to find the solution through sustainable alternatives even though the research, development, and the cost of production of these materials are costly. The sustainable development defined by values of self-reliance (empowerment and consciousness), compassion (for every creature) and renunciation of (unsustainable development and hyper-consumerism) as guided by Bharat

Ratna, Nanaji Deshmukh across the world with the backing of world superpowers, financing, and substantial lobbying and endorsement—for these biodegradable and sustainable materials will surely bring ray of hope for the generation to come with 'swaachata' being the breath of life now and eternally.

Case study: Addressing a complex problem with a multi-dimensional approach, through the implementation of a simple solution, involving several stakeholders–Sarthak an organization in Bhopal, has not only addressed the growing plastic conundrum, but successfully provided a large community of people with social securities and dignified employment, ridding them of their social taboo titles as 'waste collectors.' Sarthak Karmis earn between 100 to 150 rupees per day, granting them access to improved healthcare facilities, sponsored training and skill development programmes, and other employment opportunities in Sarthak's "vermin composting, paper making units, and recycling of plastic and other dry waste" projects. As a result of their excellent work, Sarthak was awarded the *Swachh Bharat Mission Excellence Award* in 2016 and *The Earth Care Award* in 2018.

References

https://worldcelebrityhub.com/nanaji-deshmukh-biography/Retrieved on 2 Oct. 2019.

https://www.hindustantimes.com/pune-news/nanaji-deshmukh-inspired-many-bjp-leaders-harshwardhan-khare/story-SlpRs0H8tvtNCWNOPZmcLM.html Retrieved on 1 Oct. 2019

Parker, Laura. *Planet or Plastic? We Made Plastic. We Depend On It. Now We Are Drowning In It.* National Geographic, June 2018. Web

Central Pollution Control Board (CPCB). *Life Cycle Assessment (LCA) Study of Plastics Packaging Products.* March, 2018. Web. p. 3.

Biomagnification. Merriam-Webster.com. 2009.

Toxicological Threats of Plastic. United States Environmental Protection Agency. Web

The GEF Small Grants Programme. *Community Voices—Sustainable Ways for Plastic Management.*

Venkatesh, Shreeshan, and Ishan Kukreti. "An Indian Consumes 11 kg

Plastic Every Year and an Average American 109 kg." *Down To Earth*, Centre for Science and Environment, 6 June 2018, https://www.downtoearth.org.in/news/waste/an-indian-consumes-11-kg-plastic-every-year-and-an-average-american-109-kg-60745 Retrieved on 2nd Oct., 2019.

The Energy and Resource Institute. "Fact Sheet on plastic waste in India." *The Energy and Resource Institute*, 2018, https://www.teriin.org/sites/default/files/files/factsheet.pdf Retrieved on 11 Feb., 2019.

Giacovelli, Claudia. "Single Use Plastics: A Roadmap for Sustainability." *United Nations Environment Programme*, 2018, https://wedocs.unep.org/bitstream/handle/20.500.11822/25496/singleUsePlastic_sustainability.pdf Retrieved on 11 Feb., 2019.

Kershaw, Peter. "Exploring the potential for adopting alternative materials to reduce marine plastic litter." *United Nations Environment Programme*, May 2018, http://wedocs.unep.org/bitstream/handle/20.500.11822/25485/plastic_alternative.pdf Retrieved on 11. Feb., 2019.

Parker, Laura. "We Depend On Plastic. Now, We're Drowning in It." *National Geographic*, 16 May 2018, www.nationalgeographic.com/magazine/2018/06/plastic-planet-waste-pollution-trash-crisis/#close Retrieved on 11 Feb., 2019.

"Community Voices–Sustainable Ways for Plastic Management." *Centre for Environment Education*, the GEF Small Grants Programme. 2018. Web.

16
Nanaji Deshmukh
The Great Visionary and Social Architect

Dr. Yugal Jha

Introduction

Chandika Das Amrit Rao Deshmukh, a volunteer of integral humanism and popularly known as Nanaji was a visionary, a time devoted social worker as well as political organizer developed himself as a rare example of selfless service and sacrifice par excellence in his lifetime. He was shining example of humility, honesty and austerity in the galaxy of modern politicians. He was epitome of selfless work in the field of education, health and rural self-reliance that changed the life status in the rural backward villages of our country. He was not a politician but behaved like a saint upholding high moral standard in the penumbra of today's political class. Born on 11th Oct., 1916 into a poor Marathi Deshastha Brahmin family at Kardoli village of Hingoli district of Maharashtra, when he was orphan just served and brought up by his maternal uncle to continue his education as a bright student impressed with on a scholarship by the Maharaja of Sikar.

Dr. Keshab Balram Hedgewar founder of R.S.S. was highly impressed by the zeal and devotion of Nanaji since his childhood. Nanaji Deshmukh was the first among enthused youth who proved his potential and talent to go for further higher study to Birla College (BITS, Pilani) without taking any financial support by Dr. Hedgewarji. After finishing his education, he became a full time *Pracharak* and extensively travelled all over the state for using organizational skill for the social restructuring of Indian society. His valuable contribution to the Indian society by ably discharging his responsibilities true to his words 'not me but you' as the motto of 'Mai apne liye nahi apnoke liye aya hu'. Highly impressed with the Tilak's philosophy of nation building programme and his book 'Gita Rahasya', he was nurturing the concept of integral humanism as to view of Vedic hymns explain with the rise of political social reconstruction in the context of *Sarvodaya* to *Antyodaya*. As it speaks 'Sarvye Bhawantu sukhina, Sarvye santu Niramaya'.[1] Being a highly spiritual soul, he preferred to go to serve the Indian society around the world, who are untouched by the wave of development. For Nanaji, Bharat lives in its villages where deep-seated sorrow and poverty are crippling. Thus, challenge of modern Indian society is to wipe out tears of millions surrounded, it embraces the sacred legends of rivers, mountains, forest, living and non-living organism either human or divine for the building process of Indian society.

Before Nanaji Deshmukh, one of the social reformers and saints, Swami Vivekananda voiced world to recognize it as a need of the day for the society in our global predicaments, such as economic disparities, environmental challenges and political imbalances that are not only wrong in themselves but contribute to resentments. Thus, worldwide spiritual reformative movement is very necessary to awaken the people of world for the rights and duties of each and every citizen to remove the hurdles of social-economic and political life. My effort is to explain the contribution of Nanaji for his relentless efforts to wage a revolution against languishing the people in abject poverty, misery and deprivation.

The Great Social Engineer and Performer: Nanaji Deshmukh has initiated the social engineering of rural India to upgrade the livelihood of the common people of India. To put a wide canvas for the reconstruction of socio-economic distribution of the poor people through indigenous skill with the active participant who must have vision and training of its operation for so many other avenues for the well-being of Indian society. Let the empowered people either man or women have enough skill to collect the medicinal herbs to maintain the mental health and hygiene supported by an ethics of nurturance support, caring and family responsibility. The most notable changes must be possible in the common people of society by bringing the alternative knowledge which has been preserved in the indigenous folklore to serve the nerves of society. The rural agronomy and its population have impressed with the philosophy of co-existence must have a visible expression of the divine mother, i.e. Mother India that regulates the livelihood of the common people. As the enduring filial allegiance of Vedic hymns speak "Mata Bum Putroaham Prithibiyah."[2] We in India are one-sixth of the world population and very important part of globe. What we do here with respect to education will have great impact on rest of the world. Our school, college and university are producing men and women who are highly talented and equal to best mind to search the human capital as to enkindle the practical model of *Antyodaya* and *Gramodaya* programme envisaged by the great mentor like Nanaji Deshmukh.

Nanaji was multifaceted kind-hearted personality. He was in constant search for finding goodness in mankind. As a great educationist, he was instrumental in shaping some leading educational institutions like Saraswati Shishu Mandir, Chitrakoot Gramoday Vishwavidayala, Deendayal Shodh Sansthan, Deendayal Research Institute to propagate the philosophy of Integral Humanism[3] and wanted to devote all his time for strengthening the movement for constructive work in Bharat. Incessantly he worked for the development of rural India in the principle of participation of all the public and civil society. Integral Humanism gave a vision for the Bharat that with an approach to man and his relationship to the society, i.e. integral and complementary, could transform Bharat into a self-reliant and compassionate example for the world to follow.[4]

The Great Epoch-Maker and Trend-Setter

Nanajji Deshmukh, a champion of rural development extended his distinctive poverty alleviation programme with the motto 'Har hath ko denge kam, har khet ko denge pani'[5] through the Jai Prabha Gram project in Gonda (U.P.) and Beed (Maharashtra) for surrounding villages of framers to irrigate their land. He finally launched an Integrated programme for the development of elusive area that covered health, hygiene, education, agriculture, income generation, and conservation of resources that were both sustainable and replicable. His project was done with the participatory approach for total transformation through total development with people's initiatives and participation. He was basically social reformer to empower the people's mindset for the prosperous life. Thus, envisioned his self-governance campaign to make the rural area under countless villages of India self-reliant. Nanaji Deshmukh was trend-setter with devotion and dedication to the development of weaker sections of the Indian society with the emerging innings of goodness in them defined by values of self-reliance, renunciation, penance, diligence, and compassion. Like a crusader, he did the pioneering work for the service of downtrodden people living in a beggars description for their livelihood in the remote corner of India. Nanaji was very much impressed with life persona of lord Ram. While in exile, Vanvasi Ram has changed the entire scenario of Chitrakoot with the harmonious cultural set of his life conduct. Ram has left his legacy for the *Dalit*, *Adivasi*, and women. Thus, The Vanvasi Ram has been lesson for him instead of Raja Ram.[6] Nanaji Deshmukh make Chitarkoot centre of social work to establish sound socio-cultural practices by explaining the many hymns of Vedas in a practical way for the conservation of biological and genetic diversity. In recent times, this has been forgotten or ignored in the name of elusive development. His entire workshop on poverty alleviation programme is the best panorama to understand that nature and natural resources are the great 'human entity' that we have to learn from the idealism of integral humanism that our *Rishis* and forefathers reminded us through the writings of great Epics like Vedas, *Ramayana*, and *Mahabharata*.

Nanaji was a core humanist to follow the dictum of his religious scriptures for the togetherness of Indian society as Veda speaks "Sangachya Dhayam Sambadhyam Sam wo Manasi Janatam Sewa Bhagam Yatha Purve Sanjanana Upasate". These noble thoughts became the life mode of his actions for the service of Indian society. Thus, he never runs after position and power rather he did each and every common practices for the poor people to develop their skill, attitude, crafts and livelihood for the festive culture of indigenous life. His entire efforts were dedicated as "Sa Prathama Sanskriti Vishwara". Likewise, Nanaji Deshmukh and his fine blend of political initiation challenged the dictatorial regime of the then Prime Minister Indira Gandhi during the emergency period of country. He successfully dashed against the barbaric regime and wholeheartedly supported "Sampurna Kranti" (Total Revolution) under the leadership of Loknayak Jaiprakash Narayan to pay relief to the Indian Democracy from her tyrannical despotism. During Emergency he was sent to jail for more than a year. When the Janta Party came into power, being an Member of Parliament, he rejected to be part of government rather to like work for the people of India as with the motto of their fellow-man living in a *Ashram* for value-based politics and his courage of conviction for selfless service to the poor of Indian society. Not only that while he has devoted himself for the service of poor people of India. In 1967, he crafted an alliance with socialist group by bringing together Dr. Ram Manohar Lohiya and Pt. Deen Dayal Upaydhaya—two great stalwarts committed for welfare of weaker section of society from "Sarvodaya to Antyodaya" to uplift the rural areas of India where 'Bharat Mata lives.'

The Great Educationist and Motivator: Nanaji was great educationist and motivator. He worked shoulder to shoulder to establish Pt. Deendayal's Ideology of Integral Humanism into a reality to usher in composite development of village society. He was instrumental in shaping hundred and thousand institutions of great repute for the propagation of Deendayal's philosophy of Integral humanism for reconstructing the ancient education system that represents a harmonious partnership with co-existence with nature and human life. Nanaji initiated the old pattern of education to mould India with the ancient Indian Institution like *Gurukul*[7]—Basic unit of Indian education as per the merit of soil of India. His path-breaking ideas can be very well understood the shadow of old age couple called them *Samaj Shilpi Dampati*. The groups of 20-25 students under the guidance of *Gurumata* and *Gurupita* will be brought up under the care for their all-round development. Nanaji Deshmukh introduced Chitrakoot model of experiment for couples for the whole of India to stay and work in village for a period of five years to grant the villagers social, cultural and scientific knowledge that they achieved with the long span of life. It is his effort that primary institution and higher institution with so many credible instructions for constant training and updating of knowledge in different technology had already been established in his rural university. Not only that these are being imparted with the effort of his great vision and his guidance to reorient the content and curriculum in his experiment model either in Chitrakoot or Gonda and Beed where he installed his developmental project for the uplift of rural population of India. The students learnt astronomy for acquiring knowledge of the sun, learnt grammar for understanding Veda, learnt *yoga* for health, hygiene and God, learnt the science to understand nature and life science. Learn Vedic *lokniti* for good-governance and learn foreign science for administration and well-being of the universe.

Nanaji was great motivator for building powerful blend of humanitarian constitution of one nation based on friendship, fellow-feelling, freedom and fearlessness in thought and action which are immortal and ever inspiring to the basic theology and technology of building impregnable defenses of peace in the mind of millions of people of the country. As a motivator, he concludes, 'saint and sages of all faith have been telling us that education means to love and affection, contentment and honesty. It all acquires truthful speech and knowledge coupled with practice for learning science of humanity, modest behaviour and benevolence to all. As Vedas mention:

"Vasudhev Kutumbakam"

A Great Humantarian and Leader: Nanaji Deshmukh was great humanitarian with sustainable model of development for lower middle class society and lower urban middle class people of India. He was explaining his model with spiritual economic operations with well-being of the commoners by taking subtle peep into the religious rituals and practices of rural villages of India. Of course, he was a humanitarian and always practiced his principles to grow up mentally, physically and culturally. Nanaji was facilitator-cum-leader who has combined liberal modernity that revolved around holistic development for the sufferers, poor and ignorant people of India rather than Western concept of social service that came to India because of Industrialization. He tried his best to enkindle the human consciousness to realize its inherent potential and talent to avail the alternative knowledge as per their skill, innovation and evocation. It was training and professionalism that prepared the poor people of India for their skill of growing, spinning, weaving, dyeing, printing and embroidering of cotton that Indian Crafts found their richest expression for their prosperous life.

Conclusion

Nanaji Deshmukh was the great face of self-reliance and self-governance. He was man of active habit with the dream giving employment to every villager, irrigation to every field, indigenous skill and training to each and everyone and shelter to every orphan born in debt and poverty. There is a spiritual conversation which has been carried out in the spirit of social work that Nanaji Deshmukh developed and improved for all the living and non-living organism in the premise of his rural university. His great torch bearer was *rishis* and sages which flourished into the land of Bharatvarsha—the land south to Himalayas—enriched and contextualized this great knowledge of holistic and sustainable development as per requirement of their age. The former President of India Dr. A.P.J. Kalam writes "what the octogenarian leader was doing at Chitrakoot should be an eye-opener for other and should be taken as model school which he started throughout the country namely 'Education for all: Nanhi Duniya' and octagonal shape of class room."[8]

Praising Nanaji Deshmukh on his birth anniversary 11th Oct., 1918, Dr. Bishnu Mohan Dash said, "It is historic moment for social work fraternity in India. He further added, "Deshmukh is known for his pioneering contribution towards anti-poverty, rural health, rural education, cottage industry and development for tribal population in Chitrakoot. He carried out social restructuring programme in and around remote corner of India." Nanaji Deshmukh was made first chancellor[9] of Chitrakoot Gramodaya Vishwavidayalaya in Chitrakoot, first rural university of India. He discharged his all duties and fulfilled all his responsibility as great humanitarian and communicator with devotion and skill and of course, with the ampere of a practical minded man.

On the occasion of Sharad Purnima, his birthday was celebrated on 11th Oct., 1918. He was awarded "Padma Vibhusan" in 1999. Nanaji passed away on 27th February, 2010 in the premises of Chitrakoot Gramodaya Vishwavidayalaya. He was great social reformer of our nation. He was posthumously awarded with the honour of "Bharat Ratna"[10], the highest civilian award by the Government of India in 2019.

Notes

1. "Vedic Education in India" by B.M.N. Murti, *Aryan Heritage*, June 2011, pp. 07-08.
2. Thinker of Modern India 'Need for the hour' by Gokulmurti Narayan Swami, *Dialogue*, vol. 17, Sept. 2012, pp. 75-76.
3. Deshmukh Nanaji, 2018, *Virat Purush Sakshat Nanaji*, p. 146.
4. *Manthan*, January 1996.
5. Last Vasiyat of Nanaji Deshmukh.
6. *Manthan*, January 1996.
7. Desh Mukh Nanaji, 1918, *Virat Purush Sakhsat Nanaji*, p. 146.
8. Rashtra Rishi Nanaji, Prabhat Prakashan, Delhi.
9. *The Hindustan Times*, 10th March, 1991.
10. *The Hindustan Times*, 5th October, 2019.

References

Deshmukh, N. (2018). *Virat Purush Rajnitigya Nanaji*. New Delhi: Prabhat Prakashan.

Das, B. (1977). "Emergency provisions in the Indian Constitution: A Study in Comparative Analysis". *The Indian Journal of Political Science*, pp. 237-252.

Swaroop, Devendra, *Deshmukh, Yadavrav* (2017). *Rashtra-Rishi Nanaji*. New Delhi: Prabhat Prakashan.

Thapar, R. (1977). "Inside the Janta Party". *Economic and Political Weekly*, Sept. 13, 2018.

Das Kumar and Shukla, *Social Work in India—Indigenous Approaches and Models*, pp. 4-13, Concept Publishing Company Pvt. Ltd., 2020, New Delhi.

Shah, "Revolution, Reform, or Protest? A study of the Bihar Movement: II" *Economic and Political Weekly*, pp. 642-655.

Index

Aarogya Dhaam, 126–27
Abandoned Mission of Social Work, 58
Adharmic misconduct, 111
Adivasi, 171
Agrarian
    communities, 14
    movements, 75
Agriculture/Agricultural, 26, 46, 69, 108, 125, 151
    development, 40
    land reform movement, 90
    model, diversified, 84
    Science Centre, 39–40
    insurance market, 72
    scientists, 83
Agro-climatic conditions, 71
All-inclusive expansive vision, 2
Ambedkar Social Philosophy, 153
American Model of Social Work, 59
Anamdas Ka Potha, 5
Ancient Indian knowledge, 37, 150, 162
Antarrashtriya Hindi Vishwavidyalaya, 3
Anti-poverty, 22, 75, 123, 174
Antyodaya, 36, 67, 130, 134, 169–170, 172
Aristotle, 9
Arogyadham, 39, 40, 70, 79, 109, 124, 127
Asahyoga, 119
Ashram, 39, 47, 48, 85, 86, 172
Astronomy, 173
Atharvaveda, 103
Atmanirbhar Bharat, 18, 40
Aushastipada, 6–7, 10
Ayurveda, 6, 70, 79, 93, 126–27
Ayurvedic, 70, 79, 127

Baba Amte, 31, 34
Bach, Richard, 17
Bahujan Hitaya Bahujan Sukhay, 36
Bai Deshmukh, Madam Durga, 14
Bal Jagat, 39
Bangladesh Model of Micro financing in India, 18
Basic unit of Indian education, 172
Batter plastic waste strewn, 161
Bhagavad Gita, 1, 2, 4, 14, 15, 98, 99, 102, 119
    management models of, 2
Bharat Mata, 12, 172
Bharat Ratna, 3, 6, 14, 19, 43, 72, 94, 130, 132, 156, 160, 175
Bharat-centric curriculum, 3
Bharatiya Jan Sangh, 22, 28, 129
Bharatiya models of social work, 42
Bharatiya Samaj Karya Diwas, 36, 132
Bharatiya Samaj Karya Parishad, 3, 7, 10, 12, 33
Bharatiya Shikshan Mandal, 1, 7

Bharatiya Social Work Education, 43
Bharatiya, 1–3, 7, 8, 10–12, 22, 28, 33, 36, 42–43, 48, 50, 95, 119, 129, 132, 160
Bharatiyakaran, 2, 6, 10–11, 31, 34
Bharatiyata, 111
Bharatvarsiya Sadhumargi Jain Sangh, 25
Bhartiyakaran, 50, 54
Bhave, Vinoba, 6, 22, 36, 77, 90, 129, 132, 142
Bhishma, 9
Bhoodan Movement, 22, 31, 77, 110, 129, 142
Bihar Sangharsh Movement, 28
Bio magnification, 161
Blamed consumerism culture, 138
Buddhist communities, 112
  power in, 112

Cane and Bamboo craft and Computer training, 109
Capabilities approach, 153
Capitalism, 56, 117, 136
Care models, 48
Casework Relationship, 133
Catalano, Bruno, 31
Central Pollution Control Board, 159
Chandrachood, Justice, 95
Charities, 13, 44, 59, 74, 102–3
Chipko movement, 31
Chitarkoot centre of social work, 171
Chitrakoot experiment, 16, 20, 29–31
Chitrakoot Gramoday University, 37, 162
Chitrakoot Gramoday Vishwavidyalaya, 23, 25, 27, 46, 76, 79–80, 90, 124, 130, 143, 170, 174–75
Chitrakoot initiatives, 14
Chitrakoot Model, 31, 45, 62–63, 65, 67, 69, 71, 88, 150, 172
Chitrakoot Project, 74, 78–79, 107–8, 137, 143–44
Chitrakoot *Ras Shala*, 85
Choice Based Credit System (CBCS), 1
Civil societies, 47, 154, 163–64, 170
Clean India, 157
Climate change, 66, 68, 148
Colonial India, 75
Colonialism, 106
Communalism, 76, 117
Communism, 136
Communists, 12
Community, 34, 57–59, 65, 72, 86, 119, 132–33, 136–37, 144, 146, 158, 163–64
  academic, 59
  advocacy, 145
  basis, 65
  large, 166
  local, 106, 133
  novel, 106
  religious, 106
  scientific, 161
  sustainable, 62
Community development, 25, 33–36, 40, 132–37, 139
  models of, 33–34
  rural, 134, 145
  sustainable, 34
Community mobilization, 164
Community organization, 30, 34, 77, 133
Community participation, 31, 35, 37, 67, 162
Community practitioners, 34
Concept
  dharma, 104
  ethical, 146
  innovative, 143
  modern, 62
  noble, 48
  positive, 8
  sociological, 77
  theoretical, 137
Conception, liberal, 152
Conflict resolution, 133, 138
Conflict-free society, 89, 137

Congress government policies, 129
Conscience, 52, 54
Constructive work, 38, 40, 42, 49, 93, 170
Consumerism, 43, 142
Corporate social responsibility (CSR), 137, 150
COVID-19, 64
  sustainable development and, 64
Cultural revivalism, 56

Dadhichi Dehdaan Sanstha, 23
Daivasura Samvad Vibhag Yog, 14
Dalit, 171
Dandi namak satyagraha movements, 31
Dattopant Thengadi, 56–57
Deen Dayal Research Institute, 70, 93, 124, 129, 137
Deendayal Research Institute (DRI), 7, 24, 26–27, 40, 45, 48, 70–72, 83, 87, 90, 107–9, 124–25, 129, 142–45, 150–51
Democratic Socialism, 54
Deshmukh, Amrit Rao, 18
Developmental models, 143
Dharma, 9–10, 24, 56, 98, 104, 105, 111–12, 144
Dharma Rajya, 9
Dispute-free villages, 138
Documentation centre, 127

Earth Care Award, 166
Economic conditions, 79, 82, 134–35
Economic determinism, 58
Education (Gurukul), 108
Entrepreneurship Development (Udyamita Vidyapeeth), 109
Ethical Professionalism, 7
Ethnocentricism, 60
European Imperialism, 52
Extreme weather conditions, 158, 161

Famine conditions, 75
Fernandes, George, 94
Flexner, Abraham, 160
Functionalism, 59–60

Gandhi, Indira, 172
Gandhian movement, 119
Gram Swaraj, 18–19, 74, 150
Gramdaan, 42, 111
Gramdan movement, 111
Gramodaya, 24–27, 36, 39, 44, 46, 76, 79–80, 84, 90, 110, 123–24, 126, 130, 143, 162, 170, 174, 175
Gross Domestic Product (GDP), 82, 135
Gurukul, 39, 47–48, 71, 84, 108, 118
Gurumata, 48, 172
Gurupita, 48, 172
Guru-shishya, 47

Harsh climatic conditions, 161
Hazare, Anna, 34
Health and Hygiene (*Dadi Ma Ka Batua*), 108, 127
Hinduism, 98, 106
Hindurastra, 106
Hindutva, 90, 92, 98, 106
Historic Hindu society, 112
Holistic
  approach, 59, 62, 116
  models, 37, 78, 107
Human rights, 153
Humanism, 52–53, 56, 58, 144
  internal, 135
  universal, 60
Humanitarian drive, 99, 101
  application of, 101
  performance of, 100
Hyper-consumerism, 165

Ideal villages, 134
Idealism, 93, 171
Imperialism, 52
India Today, 43, 48, 142
Indigenous knowledge, 42, 43, 115
Individualistic

approach, 58, 119
aspirations, 158
Individual-oriented
ameliorative, 76
approach, 77
Integral humanism, 37, 40, 42, 44–45, 52–57, 59–60, 78, 111, 115–18, 121–22, 124, 135–36, 150–51, 155–56, 168–72
architect of, 37
doctrine, 135–36
ideology of, 172
implementing sustainable, 163
imprints of, 37, 163
philosophy of, 23, 40, 44–45, 76, 78, 123, 130, 170, 172
self-reliance and, 111
social work and, 115–16, 121
social work model of, 149, 156
theory of, 118, 143
Integrated models, 162
Integrated Rural Development Programme (IRDP), 67
International Association of Schools of Social Work, 133
International community, 148, 154
International Day of Yoga, 12
International Federation for Women in Agriculture, 26
International Federation of Social Workers, 133
International human rights cooperation, 155
International system advancement, 154
isms, 56, 117

Jan Sangh, 56, 72, 89–90, 92–93, 142
Janata Party, 4, 27–28, 77–78, 142
Janata Party Movement, 142
Janoddarana, Deena, 29
Jawahar Gram Samridhi Yojana (JGSY), 67
Jay Prabha Village, 38
Jayaprabha Gram, 44
Jeevanvritis, 94
JP Movement, 28
Junior the Indian root was neglected, 120

Kalam, Abdul, 146
Karma Bhoomi, 18
Karma Yoga, 2, 98
Karmyogi, 93
Knowledge-based technologies, 66
Krishi Vigyan Kendras (KVK), 71, 108

Land reform movement, 111
Langar, 119
Laws of People, 153
Local geographical conditions, 66

Mahabharata, 2, 9, 171
Mana, 100
Mandela, Nelson, 120
Marathi Brahmin family, 128
Margdarshak, 21, 141
Marine organisms, 161
Marxism, 117
Marx's stateless society, 8
Millennium Development Goals (MDGs), 67, 149
Missionary activities, 106
Mixed nationalism, 55
Model educational system, 71
Modern research activities, 110
Modi, Narendra, 19
Moral idealism, 152
Mother India, 170
Muddy villages, 14
Mysterious conditions, 56
Mysticism, 52

Nagpur, 18–19, 124, 150
Nalanda of Indian Social Work, 31
Nanaji model of community development, 33
Narayana Sewa, 100
National Citizens Award, 25
National Day of Professional Social Work, 30–31

National Democratic Alliance, 137
National Mahatma Gandhi Award, 25
National Rural Employment Programme (NREP), 67
National Social Work Day, 3, 7, 12, 132
Natural law, 152
Naturopathy, 70, 79, 126
Neo-world class art, 31
Niswarth Sewa, 119
Non-biodegradable plastics, 163, 165
Non-Governmental Organizations (NGOs), 26–27, 49, 93, 142, 155, 164
Non-living organisms, 169, 174
Nussbaum, Martha C., 153

Ocean of
  human service, 17
  Indian society, 120
  service, 17
Out-door conditions, 85

Padma Vibhushan, 23, 25–27, 72, 75, 80, 89, 130
Panchjanya, 21, 24, 141
Paragon of Service, 123, 127, 129
Parmanand Ashram Paddhati Vidyalaya, 39, 86
Patriotism, 94–95
Peasant movements, 75
Political activities, 24
Political banks, 2
Political liberalism, 153
Politics to Social Work, 43
Primary Education and Primary health, 148
Principle of Social Work, 52
Profession of Social Work in India, 15
Raja Yoga, 2
Rajo-guna, 53
Ramakrishna Mission, 5
Ramayana, 2, 120, 171
Ramnath Ashram, 47–48
Ramrajya, 119–20
Rashtradharma, 21, 141
Rashtriya Swayamsevak Sangh (RSS), 4, 6, 20–21, 29, 55, 72, 90, 92, 95, 106, 128–29, 141
Rashtrodaya, 44
Rawls, John, 136, 153
Reform Movements and Hindu Sangathan, 105
Religious movements, 75
Religious universalism, 54
Revivalist movements, 106
Revolution movement, 24
Revolutionary movement, 18, 44
Richmond, Mary, 74
Rig Veda, 103
Rishis, 53, 98, 100, 171, 174
Roosevelt, Franklin D., 154
Rotary International, 94
Roy, Raja Rammohun, 53
Rural children, 71
Rural community, 34, 66, 72, 149
Rural Landless Employment Guarantee Programme (RLEGP), 67
Rural Self-Reliance and Udyamita, 127
Rural villages, 173

Sadhana, 5–6
Saha Prant Pracharak, 20
Samaj Shilpi Dampati (SSD), 48–49, 78–79, 83, 107, 138, 143, 172
Samaj Shilpis, 79
Samta Award, 25
Sanatan Dharma, 111
Sanatan, 111
Sanathan Arsha Dharma, 13
Sangathan, 106
Sangh ideology, 21, 128
Sangh Shakhas, 21, 128–29
Sanskrit word, 97–98
Saraswati Shishu Mandir, 21, 39, 47, 72, 77, 126, 129, 170
Sarthak Samudayik Vikas Evam Jan Kalyan Sanstha, 164
Sarve Bhavantu Sukhinah, 36
Sarvodaya, 6, 36, 111, 134, 169, 172

Sattva-guna, 53
Sattva-guni, 53
Satyagraha movement, 91
Satyagraha, 31, 91, 119
Satyagrahis, 91
Savarkar, 6, 106
Schools of Social Work, 30
Scientific approach, 59
Sculptors of Society, 48
Second World War, 154
Seeds for needs initiative, 71
Seeds for Social Work professionals, 15
Self Help Groups (SHGs), 71, 79, 81, 164
Self-sufficient villages, 8, 89
Sen, Amartya, 153
Settlement movement, 74
Seva Bharati, 6
Sewa, 97–107, 109, 162, 171
Sewa dharma, 98, 101–102
Sewajyoti, 104
Sewakarta, 104
Shishyas, 47
Single use plastics, 160
Skill development centre, 87
Social action model, 74
Social activities, 71, 124, 128
Social cohesiveness, 117–18, 121
Social conditions, 77
Social protest movements, 75
Social work
    approach, 133
    model of integral humanism, 153
    perspective, 50, 140
    professionalism, 35
Social Worker Educators, 49
Socialism, 56, 116–17
Socialistic Pattern of Society, 149
Spiritual reformative movement, 169
Sustainable agriculture, 46, 68–69, 84, 125, 151
Sustainable Development Goals, 63–64, 149–50
Sustainable Village Development Model, 69
Swachh Bharat Abhiyan, 157, 159, 161, 165
Swachh Bharat Mission Excellence Award, 166
Swamlamban abhiyaan, 49
SWOT analysis, 160

Tagore, Rabindranath, 29, 134
Tana, 100
Tata Energy Research Institute, 94
Technical Vocational Training, 46, 125, 151
Theoretical knowledge, 35
Theory of Justice, 136, 153
Third World, 59
Tilak, Lokmanya, 77, 116, 123
Toxicological Threats of Plastic, 161
Traditional artisans, 127
Training of Rural Youth for Self Employment, 67
Tribal children, 19, 92
Tribal villages, 86
Tyrannical despotism, 172

Udyamita, 39, 108–9, 127
United Nations Conference on Environment and Development, 63
United Nations Conference on Sustainable Development (UNCSD), 148
United Nations High Commissioner for Human Rights, 154
United Nations Sustainable Development Goals, 157
United States Environmental Protection Agency, 161
Universal Declaration of Human Rights, 152–53
Upadhyaya, Deen Dayal, 21–22, 27, 36, 40, 44–45, 56–57, 78, 100, 107, 111–12, 116, 128–30, 141, 143
Upanishadas, 5
Utilitarianism 153

Vaishwaanar, 5

Vajpayee, Atal Bihari, 22, 29, 93–94, 129, 141
Vande Mataram, 90
Vasudhaiva kutumbakam, 18, 118
Vedic hymns, 169–70
Vidyapeeth, 25, 39, 81, 109, 127
Village development, 66–67, 69, 134, 162
Village development model, 91
Village knowledge, 83
Village models, 134
Village panchayat, 150
Village self-resilient, 137
Villagers access health, 48
Virat Purush, 47
Vishwaguru, 12
Vivekananda, 5–8, 10, 12, 26, 53, 100, 121, 169

Water Conservation and Alternative Industrialization, 46, 125, 151
Water shortages, 68, 72, 74
Welfare Economics, 18, 31
Western concept of social service, 173
Western ethnocentrism, 53
Western ideals, 54
Western knowledge, 115–17, 121–22
Western models, 35, 59
Western organizational models, 106
Western philosophies, 53, 117, 119
Western society, 121
World class research centre, 126
World Monitoring Report, 67, 149
World Summit on Sustainable Development, 63

Yaganukul Educational Reconstruction, 84
Yajna, 118
Yatras, 106
Yuddhasva vigatajvara, 1